The village of Mardale Green in the mid-nineteenth century.
The valley was flooded in the 1930s to create the reservoir of Haweswater.

ROCKS AND RAIN, REASON AND ROMANCE

THE LANDSCAPE, HISTORY AND PEOPLE OF THE LAKE DISTRICT

DAVID HOWE

Saraband

Published by Saraband
Digital World Centre, 1 Lowry Plaza
The Quays, Salford, M50 3UB
www.saraband.net

10 9 8 7 6 5 4 3 2 1

ISBN: 9781912235353
ISBNe: 9781912235360

Printed and bound in Great Britain by Clays Ltd, Elcograf S.p.A.

Descriptions of sites, paths and walking trips do not imply that access
is permitted, nor that these are safe places for inexperienced visitors,
in terms of terrain, weather conditions, tides and other hazards.
Always check before travel whether visits are permitted and/or safe.
No responsibility for safety can be assumed by the author or publisher.

Title page: Grasmere, where, it is often said, Lakeland tourism began.

CONTENTS

1   Ups and Downs.. 1

2   Atoms 6

3   Rain... 14

4   Nature and the Romantics 18

5   Three Persons and One Soul 25

6   Love and More Romance 32

7   Friends, Family and Fame.............................. 43

8   Lakes 53

9   An Ocean, Ancient and Deep 63

10   Volcanoes 69

11   Mountain Building 79

12   Ice... 88

13   Stone Age to Iron Age 96

14   Roman Roads to Victorian Railways 104

15   Where to Go and What to See 120

16   Love Letters to the Lake District..................... 135

17   A Force of Nature 143

18   Back to Nature.. 156

19   Hedgehogs and Herdwicks 168

20   A National Property 178

21   Tales and Sails.. 186

22   Intimations of Mortality 197

    Bibliography 202

    Acknowledgements 207

    Index 208

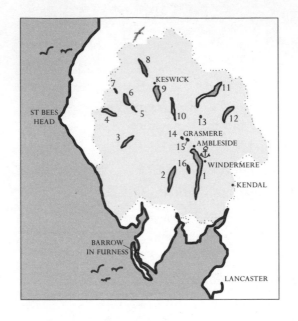

PRINCIPAL LAKES, MERES AND WATERS

1 Windermere
2 Coniston Water
3 Wastwater
4 Ennerdale Water
5 Buttermere
6 Crummock Water
7 Loweswater
8 Bassenthwaite Lake
9 Derwent Water
10 Thirlmere
11 Ullswater
12 Haweswater
13 Brotherswater
14 Grasmere
15 Rydal Water
16 Esthwaite Water

For Elsa and Lucy

Chapter 1

UPS AND DOWNS

We tumbled out of the Humber Super Snipe, stretched our legs and looked up at the hills. They rose encouragingly on either side of the valley. The thin, grey clouds began to lift. It was a late March morning. The year was 1964. Phil had recently passed his driving test and borrowed his dad's car – big, definitely new, and rather posh.

Keen to go on a long drive, Phil came up with the idea of motoring up to the Lake District for the day and invited the three of us to join him. We were seventeen and game. This would be my first visit to the Lakes.

'Helvellyn,' said Phil. 'Let's climb Helvellyn.'

'OK. Sounds good.'

Helvellyn. A mountain somewhere in the middle of the Lake District was about as much as I knew. I'm not sure that Phil or the others knew much more. The drive from our home town of Altrincham took us through the western fringes of Manchester along the A6. There were bits of the first new motorways to help us on our way. They were still a novelty. There were relatively few cars, fewer lorries and no speed limits. On one stretch we touched 100mph, just for a minute or so, because we could and the car would, with ease. And we were young.

The only map we had with us was a folded paper Shell road map. We drove past Windermere, through Ambleside and on to Grasmere, and by mid-morning we had reached the southern end of Thirlmere. The map lacked contours but it did suggest that the summit of Helvellyn was somewhere high up on our right as we motored along the A591. Looking back, we hadn't a clue.

We had just passed a signpost. It pointed up a hillside track. That would do. Phil parked the car, and out we fell. The ground was damp but not too boggy. We wore our everyday shoes. I had on my old donkey jacket hoping it wouldn't rain. The lower path ran through a wood. The route was steep – or so it seemed to four boys from the flat, suburban sprawl of south Manchester.

I can't remember too much of the climb. We soon left the trees behind and I had that thrill of suddenly seeing the world from up high. Low clouds came and went. But we made it. The broad, round-shouldered top of Helvellyn. That was the moment I fell in love with the hills, the crags, the lakes, the rivers. I was transfixed, transported. The feelings of wonder that the mountains and sky had evoked in me were, of course, by no means original. Nevertheless, that day, that moment high on the summit of Helvellyn marked the beginnings of my own love for the Lake District.

Over fifty years later I now know that the path we took must have followed Comb Gill, around Comb Crags and High Crag before levelling out onto the southern approach to Helvellyn's summit, 3,120 feet, 950 metres above sea level, the third highest peak in England. By mid-afternoon we began to make our way down. Our shoes were battered and our trousers muddy. Below us was Thirlmere. And as geography at school had been one of my favourite subjects, I did know one or two things about the lake.

Well the first thing, I suppose, is that it isn't technically a lake anymore. It's now a reservoir. A smaller, less deep lake originally ran north–south along the valley, draining via St John's Beck to join the River Greta before flowing through Keswick. The lake narrowed and shallowed in the middle creating a waist of water only a few dozen yards across. A small wooden bridge spanned this 'waist'. In dry summers when the water levels were low, the lake bed beneath the bridge would be exposed leaving two lakes on either side of the crossing. A short river-like channel ran between the two stretches of water.

The growing thirst of the growing cities of the industrial North led to various plans to dam rivers and flood small lakes to create reservoirs. The idea was not popular with the locals, particularly those with a romantic outlook and an aesthetic sensibility. John Ruskin, the sage, art critic and hater of all things ugly, said that Manchester 'should be put at the bottom of the Lake of Thirlmere.' However, in spite of local opposition, Manchester Corporation eventually was granted, by Act of Parliament, permission to tap the waters of Thirlmere. Between 1890 and 1894 a dam was built at the northern end of the lake. And slowly the waters rose, flooding the shoreline fields and lakeside woods. Also drowned beneath the rising waters were the little villages of Wythburn and Armboth.

Thirlmere reservoir is nearly four miles long. At its deepest, when the weather has been wet, its waters plunge 130 feet (40 metres). And each day it supplies Manchester and its surrounding towns with over 10 per cent of their daily thirst for water.

* * *

Here I am now, back on Helvellyn, some 50 years and more after my first trudge up the mountain, looking down on the reservoir, its black waters splintered into a million shards of sparkling summer sunshine. And a thought occurs.

Manchester is a long way south of the Lakes. How on earth, I wondered, do millions of litres of water get, every day, to the homes, offices and factories of those distant cities and towns? All I could see, in the far distance, was the northern edge of the reservoir and what I guessed was St John's Beck draining north, while Manchester lay far to the south, over 80 miles away.

As luck would have it, a few weeks after this late summer mountain-top ponder, United Utilities ('*helping life flow smoothly*') decided to celebrate the 120th anniversary of the Thirlmere Aqueduct, first opened on 12 October 1894. This is the aqueduct that takes the water all the way from the reservoir to Manchester, a distance of more than 83 miles. Starting in 1886 it took Manchester Corporation Water Works eight years to build. It's essentially a very large, very long pipe, mostly buried underground or tunnelled through rock. It is big enough for a man to stand inside, upright.

On leaving Thirlmere, the aqueduct sneaks below Helvellyn, skirts just to the east of Grasmere and Ambleside, south of Troutbeck and on to the eastern edges of Kendal. As I've climbed Heron Pike or wandered through the woods from Ambleside to Troutbeck, I must have crissed and crossed the aqueduct below my feet dozens of time without knowing it. Where on earth, or rather where under the earth, is it? Well, you can explore the aqueduct's route from start to finish, in all its splendour, on the Hidden Manchester Map website (hidden-manchester.org.uk).

On its stately way it flows, swerving east by Lancaster, Preston, Chorley, before diving to the south of Bolton. There are the occasional inspection hatches and bridges for the pipes as they cross rivers and valleys, but to the innocent eye, this extraordinary piece of Victorian engineering is all but invisible.

I'm struck by the distance the water has to travel before it gets to where it's needed. It was certainly a challenge to the Victorian engineers, but the answer lay in their knowledge of simple physics. The waters from Thirlmere to Manchester flow their great distance *entirely by gravity*. So long as the beginning of the aqueduct is higher than the end, which it is, then water will flow downhill, down the pipe, slipping, ever so slightly, down the contours. There are no pumps along the way, even though the pipe rises up and drops down on its journey south. If there are more downs than ups, then the water will flow. On average, the aqueduct falls a mere 20 inches (50 centimetres) a mile, but this is enough to keep the water flowing at a steady walking pace. And just over a day and a half after leaving Thirlmere, the water arrives at the northern fringes of Manchester, somewhere near Bolton at Lostock water treatment works.

The sheer chutzpah of those Victorian engineers beggars belief. And then another thought. As the raindrops, of which there were many that day on the fells, trickled off my jacket, soaked into the ground, seeped down the hill, and burbled into becks, they eventually found their way into the reservoir. And from there, all the way to Manchester. And who knows, hopefully after a bit of filtering and cleaning, those raindrops dripping off my waterproofs on a wet Helvellyn day, might be the very ones that eventually splurted through your tap, into your glass, before being gulped by you – that is, if you live down Manchester way.

Alfred Wainwright described a similar line of thought but one less romantic and altogether more delinquent. In his memoirs he tells us that in obeying the calls of nature, he has peed on every square mile of Lakeland, including 'with special satisfaction in Manchester's gathering grounds.' Alfred! Really, I mean to say.

Chapter 2

ATOMS

The industrial cities of the North-west have acted as a powerful gravitational force not just on Lakeland's waters, but also on its people. Throughout the eighteenth and nineteenth centuries, the cities pulled in men and women from the farms and villages to work in the factories and mills. As well as the cities' thirst for water, there was a hunger for labour too. Times were changing. The rhythm of the seasons was being replaced by the tyranny of the factory clock.

As a twelve-year-old girl my maternal grandmother, Edith, left Weston, her small Cheshire village, to go into service in Manchester thirty miles away. She left home and her family. Her father was a quiet, gentle man who looked after the plough horses on the farm where he had worked since he was a boy. He had never been much further than Crewe, a mere four miles from where he had lived and worked all his life.

The villages and hamlets of the Lake District were not immune to this urban pull. Factory workers and entrepreneurs, water and food were all sucked into the growing cities. And intellectual talent, too, was beginning to make its way south.

One of the more remarkable Cumbrian exports of the industrial revolution was John Dalton. Like the waters of Thirlmere, he slowly made his way from his Cumberland home to end up living in Manchester. He became famous for having a very big idea about a very small thing, and changed the face of chemistry for ever.

John Dalton was born on 6 September 1766, one of six children. His father was a weaver. The family lived in Eaglesfield, a small village a couple of miles south-west of Cockermouth below the Western Fells.

He went to the local village school at Pardshaw, two miles down the road from where he lived. As well reading and writing he records that aged eleven he completed 'a course in Mensuration, Surveying, Navigation, etc.' Clearly a precocious boy, the young weaver's son, aged only twelve, began to teach in the village school where he had been taught. To supplement his modest wages he also worked on the local farms. It was while he was teaching and labouring on the land that he became friends with Elihu Robinson, a fellow Quaker and a leading figure in Eaglesfield. Robinson's wealth allowed him much leisure time and he had developed a strong interest in science. It was Robinson who first introduced the young schoolboy John not only to the joys of arithmetic and the wonders of science but also how to think mathematically, how to investigate scientifically, and how to make and record observations of the weather using measuring instruments.

In 1781, aged fifteen, Dalton moved to the other side of the Lakes to live in Kendal. He joined his elder brother as a teaching assistant at a Quaker boarding school. And in time, the brothers found themselves running the school. During the twelve years he spent in Kendal, Dalton developed from a competent mathematician and investigator to an original, ground-breaking scientist. The Kendal man who more than any other helped him make this journey was John Gough.

John Gough lost his sight from smallpox when he two years old. As a child he learned Latin, Greek and French. It was while Dalton was teaching in Kendal that he met Gough, who agreed to give the young man informal lessons in both languages and geometry, mathematics and natural philosophy. Gough, although blind, could explore and work out mathematical and scientific problems in his head. And he knew by touch, taste and smell all the plants of the Lake District. By example and instruction, he helped Dalton develop a scientific attitude to complement the younger man's natural curiosity.

Wordsworth knew Gough and admitted that the first lines of his poem 'The Excursion' were based on the blind philosopher of Kendal.

> – Methinks I see him – how his eye-balls rolled
> Beneath his ample brow, in darkness paired, –
> But each instinct with spirit; and the frame
> Of the whole countenance alive with thought,
> Fancy, and understanding; while the voice
> Discoursed of natural or moral truth
> With eloquence, and such authentic power,
> That, in his presence, humbler knowledge stood
> Abashed, and tender pity overawed.

As we'll see, the poets were affected romantically and spiritually by the beauty of the lakes and hills. Dalton and Gough were more interested in the whys and wherefores of nature. But between them, the poets and the scientists inspired a deep understanding of the world about us. While the Age of Enlightenment celebrated the power of human reason to fathom nature intellectually, the Age of Sensibility valued our ability to experience nature directly through the senses, unmediated by thought or theory. Science discovered and calculated, deduced and reasoned, seeking cause and effect. Art created, made, expressed, and realised our inner visions, our subjective consciousness. Throughout the eighteenth century, both science and sensibility, reason and romance gathered pace. It was under their banner that Immanuel Kant exhorted us to 'dare to understand'.

However, before we can begin to understand, first we need to wonder. Wonder engages our imagination and then invites us to explore, scientifically, poetically, artistically, philosophically. Our culture would be foolish, writes the Italian physicist Carlo Rovelli in 2016, 'to keep science and poetry separated: they are two tools to open our eyes to the complexity and beauty of the world'. And over two hundred years earlier Dalton was determined to do his bit to explore that beauty.

When he reached the age of twenty-seven, Dalton could no longer resist the lure and pull of the city. It was 1793 when he moved to Manchester. He was appointed as a tutor in maths and natural philosophy, or what we might now call the natural sciences, at New College. The governors were members of the Manchester Literary and Philosophical Society. Six years later, with his reputation growing, Dalton made his final career move and took employment as 'private and public teacher of Mathematics and Chemistry'. Again based in Manchester.

However, it was back in 1788, in Lakeland, that he first began his interest in meteorology. His book *Meteorological Observations* was published in 1793, but he kept a daily record of the weather for fifty-seven years. He developed theories of mist formation above lakes. He had ideas about winds and why they occur. And his first scientific paper, read in 1799, had the snappy title of 'Experiments and Observations to determine whether the Quantity of Rain and Dew is equal to the Quantity of Water carried off by the Rivers and raised by Evaporation; with and Enquiry into the Origin of Springs'.

This fascination with water in the atmosphere, and the nature of clouds and water vapour marked the beginning of Dalton's enquiries into the fundamental nature of things. After several years of looking at, measuring and thinking about vapours and gases, liquids and solvents, he came up with his atomic theory of matter. All matter

– whether solid, liquid or gas – is made up of very small things called atoms. The radii of different isolated atoms vary, but in general they range between 25 and 200 picometres, where a picometre equals a trillionth of a metre. That really is very small. This means that there are millions of trillions of atoms in just one cubic centimetre of, say, copper or carbon.

It's true that the Greeks and Indians came up with the idea that matter is made up of atoms over two thousand years earlier, but their notions were philosophical rather than scientific, and of no practical value. Dalton was saying much more. His ideas about atoms revolutionised our understanding of chemistry. His insights helped lay the foundations of the periodic table of the chemical elements, later to be developed, defined and designed so beautifully by the nineteenth-century Russian chemist Dmitri Mendeleev.

Modern-day definitions of the atom describe it as the smallest constituent of a chemical element which still retains the individual characteristics of that element. Each element – whether hydrogen or sodium, carbon or gold – is therefore made of atoms each of which has chemical and physical properties characteristic of that element.

On 21 October 1803, Dalton read a paper to the Manchester Literary and Philosophical Society. It was on this occasion that he first made the original suggestion that each element has its own defining properties, including its unique atomic weight. He said that all atoms of the same element are identical and can combine with other elements to form compounds. Over the next few years he developed and refined these profound insights. His work on the atomic theory of chemistry made him world famous, certainly among fellow scientists, and in his day among the populace at large.

Dalton also proposed that chemical compounds are combinations of two or more different types of atom. But when different atoms combine, they do so in the same proportions, no matter how they are composed. For example, the solid metal sodium (Na) and the gas chlorine (Cl) can combine to form sodium chloride (NaCl) or common salt. The proportion of sodium and chlorine in the compound are always the same, however manufactured. One atom of sodium for every one atom of chlorine. Thus, Dalton was able to say that when atoms of different elements combine to make a compound they do so in simple, whole number ratios. Therefore, all chemical reactions are just rearrangements of atoms in fixed whole number ratios to form chemical compounds. For example, when two atoms of hydrogen combine with one of oxygen we get water whose chemical formula, of course, is H_2O. When two oxygen atoms combine with one of carbon, the result is carbon dioxide (CO_2).

Dalton's understanding of atoms, compounds and their reactions fundamentally changed the way we think about chemistry. When chemists grasped his ideas of chemical atomic theory, not only did it help them make sense of what happens when different substances combine, recombine and separate, but it also opened up a world of possible new chemical compounds and substances.

The realisation that through various physical and chemical processes, men and women had the power to rearrange atoms and create new materials laid the foundation of much of the industrial revolution. The chemical and pharmaceutical industries now had a clear scientific logic to support their activities. There was the possibility of making thousands and thousands of new chemical compounds. And so, with this understanding, the world changed forever. Science began to take on a progressive role. Just look around you and so much of what we use, see, touch, taste and smell was once an experiment in a chemist's laboratory – paints and plastics, medicines and materials, disinfectants and detergents, acids and alkalis. All thanks in no small part to the son of an Eaglesfield weaver.

Dalton lived a modest life. He retained his Cumbrian accent. His habits were regular. He kept his diary of weather observations until the day before he died, which he did on 27 July 1844, aged seventy-seven. His last notes observe that there was 'Little Rain', a light SW wind, and a maximum daytime temperature of 71° F.

Forty thousand people filed past his coffin as it lay in Manchester Town Hall. A cortege of a hundred carriages and a hundred mourners on foot accompanied his body to its final resting place. Dalton was buried in Ardwick Cemetery. The cemetery, alas, is no more. It's been grassed over and is now known as Nicholls Field. There is a large sign on the edge of the park that mentions some of the famous people buried there including 'John Dalton, Scientist'. But John Dalton's granite tombstone was saved. It now lies beside his statue outside the Manchester Metropolitan University's John Dalton Building. Each year the Manchester Literary and Philosophical Society organise The Dalton Lecture, delivered by an eminent scientist of the day. The society's most distinguished award is the Dalton Medal, bestowed annually to a scientist of note. The University of Manchester, too, honoured John Dalton's pioneering work when it named its prestigious physics research facility the Dalton Nuclear Institute. Quite a record for a young boy from Lakeland.

On the corner of Dalton Lane – where else – above the door of the house in Eaglesfield where he was born is written in unpretentious rustic capitals:

JOHN DALTON DCL.LLD.
THE DISCOVERER OF
THE ATOMIC THEORY
WAS BORN HERE ON SEPT 5 1766
DIED AT MANCHESTER JULY 27 1844

John Dalton never lost his love of the Lake District, its hills and mountains. He would return there for most of his holidays, although even then he would be measuring the heights of mountains, recording the weather and wondering about the clouds. It is estimated that over his lifetime, Dalton climbed Helvellyn more than forty times. Aged sixty-six, he could still be found walking the fells, measuring air pressure, testing the humidity, and predicting whether or not it might rain.

Chapter 3

RAIN

Of course, the Lake District has more than its fair share of rain. 'The rain here,' wrote a chirpy Wordsworth, 'comes down heartily, and is frequently succeeded by clear, bright weather, when every brook is vocal, and every torrent sonorous.' Keswick enjoys nearly 60 inches (1,500 millimetres) of rain a year while Ambleside gets a soaking of up to 80 inches (2,000 millimetres) every twelve months. Seathwaite, nestling in Borrowdale, has the happy reputation of being the wettest inhabited place in England with an annual drenching of around 140 inches (3,500 millimetres).

And it's even wetter on the mountain tops. Westerly winds prevail across the British Isles. They travel thousands of miles across the Atlantic Ocean and are laden with moisture. When they hit land they rise, and, as John Dalton observed, rising air cools, the moisture condenses, clouds form and rain falls. This is why the western edges of our islands are wetter than the east. Mountains force the humid airs even higher, and so the rains are heavier.

Meteorologists call this type of rain orographic (mountain) or relief rain. Being in the west *and* rather hilly, it is no surprise that the Lake District gets a regular dousing. And by way of contrast, just in case you were wondering, the driest parts of the country, including the village of St Osyth in east Essex, are in the lowlands of the south-east of England with not a mountain in sight. Here the annual rainfall can be as little as 20 to 23 inches (500 to 600 millimetres). Almost a desert.

RAIN

Melissa Harrison was moved to write a whole book about rain – *Rain: Four Walks in English Weather*. In her introduction, she recalls, 'The idea for this book came to me in the Lake District,' before adding that the region 'has some of the highest rainfall in the entire UK, and when we go there we go prepared'.

No months are particularly dry in Cumbria. Even in May, the driest month, around 3 inches (80 millimetres) of rain falls in the valleys and on the villages. October to January, not surprisingly, are the wettest months, each with between 6 and 7 inches, 150 to 180 millimetres of rain. Yet there are days when the rain is not just heavy, but torrential, and prolonged.

Storm Desmond spilled across the North of England on the 5th and 6th of December 2015. Over 13 inches (341.4 millimetres) of rain fell across the central Lake District in just 24 hours, breaking existing records. The gills and becks cascaded down the hillsides. Rivers raged and burst their banks. Towns and villages flooded. The bridge at Pooley Bridge was one of many to be damaged or washed away. A large section of the A591 over Dunmail Raise between Grasmere and Keswick collapsed into the beck-turned-torrent that roared by the road's side. The north of the county was cut off from the south. This key route through the middle of the Lakes didn't reopen until June 2016.

As I write this, a couple of years have already passed since Storm Desmond did its worst. I'm walking up Easedale, in the rain. It's been raining all morning. Hossin' it down. But it is February. The Langdale Pikes are hidden in the low, grey cloud. Easedale Tarn is rippled by the wind and fretted by the rain. I'm with Wainwright, figuratively speaking, who famously said: 'There's no such thing as bad weather, only unsuitable clothing.' And so I am dressed in my boots, waterproof trousers and jacket. My hood is up and the rain pitters and patters against the fabric. For a moment I stop and close my eyes. The sound is primitive, elemental. I'm cocooned. I'm dry. There is no one else about. I feel myself dissolve into the swirl of the mists, the watery sky, and the ghostly presence of the cloud-cloaked mountains looming all around.

We might also say that there is no such thing as bad weather, only different weather. It's a matter of getting into the right mind-set. Now I agree if it's mid-June and you're planning a picnic on the grassy banks of Ullswater, rain isn't going to be your friend. But if you are content just to wander, by the rivers, over the fells, by the lakes, then relish skies that are wild or a sun that is setting, or rain.

The weather, whatever the weather, has its own unique effect on what we see, hear, feel, smell. For example, there is that special word for the smell of rain falling on hot, dry, dusty ground – petrichor. The word derives from the Greek *petra* for stone, and *ichor*, a golden fluid said to flow through the veins of the gods. Petrichor – the scent of rain after a long-parched summer.

Rain inspires writers and poets, thinkers and artists. It can drizzle and mizzle. It can chuck it down, throw it down and piss it down. It can be light or heavy, patchy or steady, a cloudburst or torrential. In her 1855 book, *A Complete Guide to the English Lakes*, Harriet Martineau, quoting a local resident, warns the visitor, 'It donks and it dozzles; and whiles it's a bit siftering: but it don't often make no girt pel.' Make of that what you will.

Some people become philosophical as storms lash or drizzle dampens. Lying in bed, listening to the rain rattle against the windows, is a wonderfully soothing sound for many of us. Although not apparently for Samuel Taylor Coleridge. He was staying with William and Dorothy Wordsworth at Dove Cottage in Grasmere. It had been raining all night. He was not in the best of moods. His domestic life was none too happy. And so he wrote 'An Ode to the Rain', admittedly jocular in tone. Here is the opening section:

I know it is dark; and though I have lain
Awake, as I guess, an hour or twain,
I have not once open'd the lids of my eyes,
But I lie in the dark, as a blind man lies.
O Rain! that I lie listening to,
You're but a doleful sound at best:
I owe you little thanks, 'tis true,
For breaking thus my needful rest!
Yet if, as soon as it is light,
O Rain! you will but take your flight,
I'll neither rail nor malice keep,
Though sick and sore for want of sleep:
But only now, for this one day.
Do go, dear Rain! do go away!

But if it did go away, we wouldn't have the gills and becks, rivers and streams, lakes and waterfalls. We would not have the Lakeland landscape that kept Wordsworth rooted in his home soil, or which drew Coleridge himself to settle for a while by the lakes and beneath the fells. And the Romantic enterprise would have been the poorer.

Chapter 4

NATURE AND THE ROMANTICS

The importance of Wordsworth and Coleridge and the friendship between the two men has been the subject of countless studies, and it's with a quote from Coleridge that this chapter, indeed this book, takes its inspiration. Coleridge was interested in everyone and everything. He read prodigiously. He loved to travel. Unlike Keats, who feared that Isaac Newton's experiments with light and prisms would 'unweave a rainbow', taking the poetry out of raindrops and sunshine, science and scientists interested Coleridge as much as poetry and philosophy. He met Humphry Davy and attended his Royal Institution lectures. Wonder and curiosity kept his mind busy and his body restless. As Coleridge says, in his 1817 book *Biographia Literaria; Or, Biographical Sketches of My Literary Life and Opinions*, in which he celebrates the importance of the imagination:

> To find no contradiction in the union of the old and new ...
> characterises the mind that feels the riddle of the world,
> and may help to unravel it. To carry the feelings of child-
> hood into the powers of manhood; to combine the child's
> sense of wonder and novelty with the appearances, which
> every day for perhaps forty years had rendered familiar.

Today it is hard to imagine that it was not always the case that nature and its grandeur could excite the imagination, inspire artists and heighten our very sense of being. It was not until the late eighteenth century – with the impact of the dispassionate objectivity of reason, the cold logic of science, the ugliness of industry and the relentless pull of the cities and their dirty factories – that poets and artists in Europe began to develop arguments that valued subjectivity and celebrated the imagination.

The natural landscape had the power to generate strong feelings and an awareness of one's inner world, which in turn could fire the artistic imagination. The philosopher Isaiah Berlin went so far as to say that Romanticism represented 'the greatest single shift in the consciousness of the West'. It redefined how we understand ourselves. It explored how we might live our lives. It gave us a new way of looking at the world. It recognised the depth of our relationship with nature and the environment.

Nature and the simple life became the major theme of the Romantics. The Romantic gaze was one in which the everyday objects, of nature and man, might be viewed with wonder and a strange eye, as if seen for the first time. Rivers and mountains, wind and rain, sea and sky had the power to inspire painters and poets alike. In fact, nature at its most dramatic and wild could enthral the artist, leaving him or her in a state of awe. Beneath a stormy sky, the painter J. M. W. Turner turned to address his friend Mr Hawkey, and said, 'Hawkey! Hawkey! Come here! come here! Look at this thunder-storm. Isn't it grand? – Isn't it wonderful? – Isn't it sublime?'

The Romantics introduced the idea that there was a deep, organic relationship between people and the world in which they lived. If that world was rich in beauty and natural wonders, so much the better for the spirit and the soul. But if that world was ugly and disfigured, the lives of men and women would be impoverished and imagination crushed. Contemplating nature's beauty could create feelings of inner joy. Real happiness, wrote the poet John Clare, is

'to stand and muse upon the bank of a meadow pool fringed with
reed and bulrushes and silver clear in the middle on which the sun is
reflected in spangles … this is a luxury of happiness and felt even by
the poor shepherd boy'.

The force and majesty of nature could arouse feelings so strong
in the Romantic observer that the individual could be reduced to
a state of thrilling fear and awesome wonder. To feel at one with
nature was the aim of much Romantic artistry, and Wordsworth
and Coleridge were among the first to ride the Romantic wave in
Britain. And where better to do so than in the Lake District.

Few landscape, nature or travel writers today can resist the
sublime. Their indebtedness to the Romantics runs through their
passions and prose. High on the summit of Ben Hope in the far
north-west of Scotland, on his own in the middle of winter, the
writer, walker and environmentalist Robert Macfarlane felt – and
feared – the majestic indifference of nature:

> All travellers to wild places will have felt some version
> of this, a brief blazing perception of the world's disinter-
> est. In small measures it exhilarates. But in full form it
> annihilates.

Wordsworth was born on the edges of Lakeland in 1770,
Coleridge in Ottery St Mary, Devon in 1772. Wordsworth enjoyed
the quiet life. Rumination and contemplation suited him well. In
contrast, Coleridge could talk nineteen-to-the-dozen. It was often
difficult for other people to get a word in edgeways. His interests were
wide. His mind was active, restless, febrile. He would throw himself
into new experiences with huge energy and enthusiasm. There were
no half measures. When a young John Keats met Coleridge, who by
then was nearing fifty, he recalled that they walked a mile or two,

and in those two miles Coleridge 'broached a thousand things'. But there were other times when he suffered anxiety and depression. He would take to his bed and to the drugs.

However, there were many similarities in the lives of Wordsworth and Coleridge. Wordsworth's mother died when he was just seven years old, followed by the death of his father six years later. When he was just eight, Coleridge's father, the Reverend John Coleridge died. Both boys were packed off to boarding school. Both men gained places at Cambridge University, Coleridge arriving in 1791, the year that Wordsworth left. Wordsworth scraped his degree. Coleridge didn't even manage that – in spite of his undoubted brilliance and mercurial intellect, his lack of enthusiasm for university studies ended up with him not taking his final degree. As young men, both Wordsworth and Coleridge began to write poetry.

It was not until after their Cambridge years, in 1795, that Wordsworth and Coleridge finally met. Coleridge was already friends with another young poet, the tall and gangly Robert Southey. All three men eventually met up in Bristol and clearly took to each other. They were young, radical and romantic. They hatched plans to sail off to the east coast of America and create an ideal community. That year, Southey and Coleridge married two Bristol sisters, Edith and Sara Fricker, who were initially game to join the men on their utopian adventure. In the event the American dream never happened. But what did happen was that the three men – Wordsworth, Coleridge and Southey – were destined to spearhead the English Romantic movement, living much of their lives in the Lake District. We now know them as the Lakeland poets.

* * *

William Wordsworth was born in Cockermouth on 7 April 1770, the second oldest of five children – four boys and a girl, Dorothy, born on Christmas Day 1771. John Dalton was born only four years earlier and a few miles away, but William and John, to our knowledge, never met. It seems extraordinary that two great men, one of words and one of numbers, should be playing in the fields and by the rivers of west Cumbria around the same time.

Cockermouth was then a small, provincial town with a population of about 2,600. Much of the town's work involved making hats, cloth and leather. The Wordsworths lived on the main street in a large, elegant Georgian house which backed on to the River Derwent. However, the Wordsworths didn't own the house. It was the property of Sir James Lowther. He had the reputation of being rich, ruthless, corrupt and politically ambitious. You crossed Sir James at your peril. Behind his back, many locals called him 'Wicked Jimmy' and 'Jimmy Grasp-all'. He was the biggest landowner in the whole of Westmorland and Cumberland and William's father, John, was the law agent for Sir James.

William records happy memories of his childhood. He roamed free, swam in the Derwent, and gazed at Skiddaw in the distance. He later wrote how he had 'run abroad in wantonness to sport/A naked savage in the thunder-shower'.

But his carefree days did not last. After his mother died, Wordsworth's maternal grandparents stepped in, and for much of the year they agreed to look after the young brothers at their home in Penrith. The grandmother was strict. She certainly didn't countenance wild roving let alone wild swimming. This was not a happy time for William.

Dorothy, as the only girl, was packed off elsewhere. Aged only five, she went to live in Halifax with her mother's cousin, Elizabeth Threlkeld, who appears to have been a kindly soul.

A couple of years later in May 1779, William and his older brother Richard were sent south, over the fells, to become pupils at

Hawkshead Grammar School. The school was founded in 1585 by the Archbishop of York. William came into his own here and happy days returned, only to be upset once more four years later when his father died, aged only forty-two. Although the boys continued to board at the school, now orphaned they had no choice during the holidays but to return to Penrith and their fun-sapping grandparents.

School became a haven, and it began to shape William's enthusiasms. Mrs Tyson, with whom the boys lodged, gave them extraordinary freedom to roam, wander and explore the lakes and fells for miles around.

William found the new headmaster, William Taylor, a Cambridge graduate and reverend, inspirational. Wordsworth learned Latin, Greek and arithmetic, but he was also introduced to English literature and poetry. His passion for language and especially poetry was fired. This was also the time when William first began to write poems himself, often encouraged by his long, reflective walks.

Aged 17, William went off to St John's College, Cambridge. To help pay his way, he had won one of the coveted sizar's places. This entitled him to pay reduced fees as well as enjoy free meals.

At Cambridge he continued to write his own poetry, to some extent at the expense of his more conventional studies. His youthful rebelliousness and rather headstrong character began to assert themselves ever more determinedly. He gave up attending many of the lectures and courses, preferring instead to do his own reading and learning. Nevertheless, in spite of his disillusionment with much of Cambridge life, in 1791 he graduated with a bachelor's degree, albeit without honours. Not long after, in November, he headed off to France to witness the early days of the French Revolution, the end of monarchy and the beginnings of republicanism.

However, poetry and politics were not the only things he fell in love with. While in France he also met and became captivated by Annette Vallon. Their shared passion resulted in Annette getting pregnant. Perhaps not his finest hour, Wordsworth left France before his daughter was born. He had run out of money but it was also getting increasingly dangerous for English subjects to be abroad in France. Caroline, his daughter, was born on 15 December 1792. Although William and Annette never married, Wordsworth endeavoured to stay in touch and support his little girl as best he could. But nine years would pass before he first set eyes on young Caroline.

Chapter 5

THREE PERSONS AND ONE SOUL

Dorothy's childhood stay with her aunt in Halifax was a happy one. However, she never visited the Lake District or saw her brothers while she was there. It was not until she returned as a teenager to stay with her gloomy Penrith grandparents that she was finally able to catch up with her brothers. But even that wasn't destined to last too long. Her uncle, the Reverend William Cookson, married and went off to become vicar of Forncett St Peter in Norfolk. Dorothy was invited to join them and in 1788 she headed east.

In Norfolk, she acted as a kind of housekeeper, helping to look after the children, and she took many walks by the River Tas. Cambridge was only sixty miles away and brother William came over to visit on two occasions, once in the summer of 1789 and again the following year. In 1793, the vicar learned of William's affair with Annette and the birth of their child Caroline. William was banned from making any further visits to see his sister. A moral reprobate such as William Wordsworth was no longer welcome in respectable Forncett St Peter.

Dorothy lived with the Cooksons for six years but her devotion to brother William proved too strong. They hatched a plan, in secret, to meet up in Halifax when Dorothy was on a visit to see her aunt. And it was there that they decided on a life together which began with them visiting the Lake District. Dorothy had spent very little time in her home county since she had first left for Halifax as a little girl. The date of her return was 1794.

The siblings' plan was to head for Keswick. They didn't have much money, so having reached Kendal by coach they walked the next five miles to Staveley. And the next day, they strode another twelve miles to Grasmere, where they spent the night, before marching off again to walk another fifteen miles to the far side of Keswick. This three-day hike left them tired but exhilarated. They found the scenery mesmerising. The long walk had left them breathless but so did the beauty of the mountains and lakes. 'I walked with my brother at my side ...' wrote Dorothy, 'through the most delightful country that was ever seen.'

For the next few months they lodged with friends and visited relatives. While William was busy making contacts and planning his future, Dorothy was happy to meet cousins and renew old friendships, including one with his future wife, Mary Hutchinson. For a while William went to stay in London. However, the inheritance of a small legacy allowed brother and sister the longed-for chance to live together. This, coupled with a generous offer to live rent-free by the owner of Racedown Lodge in Dorset, saw the Wordsworths move to the South West. They arrived in their large, new home on 26 September 1795.

* * *

Robert Southey was still a student at Balliol College, Oxford when he first met Samuel Taylor Coleridge, in June 1794. Both young men had an interest in politics, poetry and prose. They got on well. They continued to write individual projects but also began to collaborate on various literary ventures. It was during this time that, along with another ex-Balliol student, George Burnett, they began to excite themselves with ideas of forming a new, ideal, idealistic, experimental community over in America. They called it a Pantisocracy, a place where all would be equal.

Southey decided not to complete his university studies, a habit that seems to be a prerequisite to becoming a Romantic poet. Leaving Oxford, he returned to his native Bristol where once more he was joined by Coleridge. By late 1794, the aspiring poets and Pantisocrats were lodging together. They continued to talk of sailing west to the banks of the Susquehanna River. They had enthused several others and at one point they had gathered over twenty people, including all five of the Fricker sisters, to join them on the adventure.

As we learned in the previous chapter, Wordsworth also visited them for the first time in Bristol, and found himself caught up with their radical enthusiasms. March 1795 was to be the date the young utopians planned to sail west. But reality began to kick in. Disagreements about the social, political and economic structure of the community began to fracture relationships. Coleridge was beginning to exasperate Southey, and the idea of a new life in America was abandoned.

The poets' marriages to the two Fricker sisters meant that from time to time the two men and their families would meet, but feelings between the two poets rapidly cooled. Their contrasting personalities and habits also ensured that their literary lives took very different courses.

In 1796 Coleridge, his wife Sara and baby son Hartley moved to Nether Stowey in Somerset, not too far from Racedown Lodge in Dorset where William and Dorothy were living. However, to be even closer to Coleridge, in 1797 the Wordsworths decided to move to Alfoxton House, only three miles from Nether Stowey.

The friendship between Wordsworth and Coleridge became increasingly intense. They walked for miles, across country, up and down the Quantock Hills, talking, planning, inspiring each other. They travelled together, shared ideas, read each other's poems and fired each other's imaginations. They entered a phase of extraordinary creativity. Dorothy, too, became swept up in these animated times. Coleridge wrote that he, William and Dorothy were 'three persons and one soul'. In Dorothy and Coleridge, William found two powerful influences who would support his burgeoning life as a poet.

It was during 1797 – his *annus mirabilis* – that Coleridge wrote many of his finest and most successful poems. Most famously, they included 'The Rime of the Ancient Mariner', 'Kubla Kahn' and the beginnings of 'Christabel'.

The Somerset walks and excited conversations enjoyed by Coleridge and Wordsworth found them hatching a plan to publish a book of their radical new-style poetry. The language, they declared, would be the plain language of everyday speech. The lives they would write about would be the lives of ordinary people. The book was to be called *Lyrical Ballads*. However, it eventually fell on Wordsworth to see the project through. Only four out of the twenty-four poems to appear in the jointly authored book, Volume I of *Lyrical Ballads*, were by Coleridge, one of which was 'The Rime of the Ancient Mariner'. The verses were published in 1798. All thirty-eight poems in Volume II of *Lyrical Ballads*, published in 1800, were by Wordsworth. Oddly, the supervision and proofreading of this second volume were done by the Cornishman and budding scientist, Humphry Davy.

* * *

While living in Bristol, Coleridge and Robert Southey had also become friends with Davy. Davy was working for Dr Thomas Beddoes at Bristol's Pneumatic Institute. The institute was experimenting with various gases including nitrous oxide, better known as laughing gas, still used in anaesthetics today. All three friends had inhaled the gas, thoroughly enjoying and recommending its euphoric effects. After trying the gas Southey wrote to his brother:

O Tom! Such a gas has Davy discovered, the gaseous oxide. Oh, Tom! I have had some; it made me laugh and tingle in every toe and finger tip. Davy has actually invented a new pleasure, for which language has no name. Oh, Tom! I am going for more this evening. It makes one strong and happy! So gloriously happy!

He clearly enjoyed it. So did Coleridge, of course. However, at this stage the more sober Wordsworth had not yet met Davy. Nevertheless, Wordsworth accepted Coleridge's recommendation that Davy read and correct the proofs of the second volume of *Lyrical Ballads*. Davy was only twenty-two at the time. Wordsworth's letter to Davy, written in August 1800, should hearten all schoolchildren struggling with spelling and punctuation:

Dear Sir,

So I venture to address you though I have not had the happiness of being personally known to you. You would greatly oblige me by looking over the enclosed poems and correcting any thing you find amiss in the punctuation a business at which I am ashamed to say I am no adept … I write to request that you would have the goodness to look over the proof-sheets of the 2nd volume before they are finally struck off.

Yours sincerely,

W. Wordsworth

* * *

Modern-day scholars now regard *Lyrical Ballads* as marking the beginning of the English Romantic movement. It represented a radical shift in style from the classical, flowery language of earlier poetry. Many of the poems were about ordinary people and the natural world, all written in everyday language, all with great feeling and imagination.

It was as the first edition of the book was being published that Coleridge, William and Dorothy Wordsworth decided to go travelling in Germany. It was the autumn 1798. The venture was right up Coleridge's street. Sara, who now had two young children, was left behind. The exciting prospect of learning a new language, making new friends and having bold ideas appealed to Coleridge's gregarious, impetuous, enthusiastic nature.

The Wordsworths, too, were hoping to learn German, meet fellow writers and hear more about new developments in the natural sciences. In the event, they stayed only a year. The winter had been extremely cold, they felt tired of travelling and began to feel homesick. They were missing the lakes and fells. In December 1799, William and Dorothy decided to return to the north of England, leaving Coleridge behind in Germany. It was during one of their walks, not long after their return to the Lakes, that brother and sister spotted a small house for rent on the outskirts of Grasmere.

It was one of the cottages in the hamlet known as Town End, Grasmere. It had been an inn, the Dove and Olive Branch, on the Kendal to Keswick coach road, and over time it would become Dove Cottage. The house overlooked Grasmere's waters across to the gentle rise of Silver How and the rough and rumbly tops of Loughrigg Fell. It had been ten years since William had actually lived in the Lakes. Dove Cottage suited brother and sister fine and there they lived for the next eight years, although by no means alone. And there, wrote Dorothy, they settled to a life of 'plain living and high thinking'.

Once back in England, Coleridge began making periodic visits to the Lakes, again leaving behind Sara and his two children. He was still writing poetry and taking walks with Wordsworth. They would sometimes be accompanied by Dorothy. All three enjoyed each other's company. They talked, shared ideas, recited their poems. Indeed, they often resented any visitor who might wish to join them. Coleridge wrote, somewhat flippantly:

> We three dear friends! in truth we groan
> Impatiently to be alone.

However, the poetic trio were about to be joined by two more sisters.

Chapter 6

LOVE AND MORE ROMANCE

In 1799, not long after his return to the Lakes, William Wordsworth once more found himself in the same company as his and Dorothy's Penrith childhood friend, Mary Hutchinson. It was therefore only a matter of time before Coleridge made not only Mary's acquaintance, but also that of her younger sister, Sara. For Coleridge, Sara was love at first sight, although of course he was already married, with children, to another Sara, Sara *née* Fricker.

'For the first time,' Coleridge wrote, 'Love pierced me with its dart, envenomed, and alas! incurable.' But being a married man, and Sara Hutchinson being a respectable woman, his love was doomed, although their friendship endured. The 'gang' of five, as Coleridge was wont to call them, comprised William and Dorothy, Mary and Sara Hutchinson, and himself. And when William's younger brother John was home from sailing the seas, he too joined the gang. They walked together, admired views and rhapsodised about Nature.

Coleridge's strong feelings for Sara Hutchinson never left him, even though they would cast him into states of extreme despair. In many of his verses, he anagrammatised her name to Asra. He wrote poems for her and about her, both happy and sad. His poem, 'Dejection: An Ode', was written when he was in one of his more despondent moods. In its second draft, Coleridge declaims the power of nature and the imagination to heal grief and depression. 'Love', on the other hand, was a poem written when his state of mind was altogether more joyous. It begins:

> All thoughts, all passions, all delights,
> Whatever stirs this mortal frame,
> All are but ministers of Love,
> And feed this sacred flame.

On 29 June 1800 Coleridge again visited the Lake District and this time he brought with him his long suffering, unloved, increasingly sidelined wife, who was again pregnant. Never the easiest of guests, Coleridge's stay at the tiny Dove Cottage was by no means a short one.

For some time he had been taking the highly addictive drug opium, partly to ease his aches and pains (made worse, he claimed, by the cold, damp climate), and partly to overcome his bouts of depression, and in later years, his unrequited love. With swollen eyes, rheumatic pains and feelings of lethargy, Coleridge took to his bed. It was not until a month later that the Coleridges eventually moved out, into the rented house that Dorothy had found for them – Greta Hall in Keswick.

Marriage between William and Mary Hutchinson was clearly on the cards but there was still the matter of Annette Vallon and their daughter Caroline, now aged nine. Dorothy, always a great letter writer, had been in fairly regular correspondence with Annette over the years. Enmities between Britain and France had eased and so Dorothy persuaded William that, before he married Mary, he really ought to visit Annette and Caroline and be open and honest about where everyone now stood.

In 1802, brother and sister met mother and daughter in Calais. They spent a month together. William's forthcoming marriage was acknowledged and a small annual payment was arranged to support

Annette and their daughter. This arrangement continued until 1834 when Wordsworth made a final settlement of a lump sum of £400 on forty-two-year-old Caroline, a reasonably significant amount of money in those days.

William married Mary Hutchinson on 4 October 1802. The ceremony took place in the pretty twelfth-century Church of All Saints, Brompton by Sawdon, eight miles west of Scarborough. Coleridge didn't attend. Dorothy, too, failed to make it to the actual ceremony. For seven years, she and William had lived a close, intense life together. And now Mary was to join them. Dorothy recounts having worn Mary's wedding ring the night before, then early the next morning she returned it to William who 'slipped it again onto my finger and blessed me fervently'.

Feeling rather emotional, Dorothy took to her bed. However, she did manage to greet the couple on their return to the cottage they had hired. In her journal she writes that in spite of her weakened state, she 'forced' herself from the bed 'faster than my strength could carry me till I met my beloved William & fell upon his bosom. He & John Wilkinson led me to the house & there I stayed to welcome my dear Mary.'

Mary and Dorothy had very different personalities. Dorothy was sensitive, even fragile, physically and emotionally. Her 'sensibilities' were said to be high. She was easily moved, by people and the forces of nature. In contrast, Mary was calm, steady and accepting.

Coleridge, of course, was still around, still unhappily married to Sara, and still living at Greta Hall from the top floors of which there were magnificent views of the mountains and lakes. Not long after he first moved into the house, Coleridge wrote 'my God! what a scene!' He named their new baby Derwent, after the lake. He continued writing poetry and taking walks with Wordsworth.

Coleridge's health was getting poorer and he was growing a little envious of William's rising success. His mind, though, was buzzing as ever. His thoughts and ideas were still capable of beauty and brilliance. The biographer Richard Holmes described Coleridge's world at this time as 'a kind of glistening chaos.' Coleridge was often in London. His interests in science continued to be strong. In 1802 he attended Humphry Davy's lectures on chemistry at the Royal Institution. He recognised that both science, as refined reason, and art, as the exploration of experience, led to a better understanding of the world.

During 1803, Coleridge joined William and Dorothy Wordsworth on a tour of western Scotland. Mary, who had given birth to their first child, John, in June, stayed at home. However, not long into the trip Coleridge said he felt unwell and planned to return home. The Wordsworths went on without him but later discovered that Coleridge in fact had not left Scotland. A quick recovery found him travelling the Highlands on his own, clearly enjoying himself. In a letter to his wife he wrote that he was managing to walk many miles a day, and that his spirits were high 'having found myself so happy alone'.

Touring in an altogether more leisurely fashion, on their way home through the Scottish Borders, William and Dorothy called in to see Walter Scott. He was younger than the Wordsworths and was still several years off the height of his fame as a novelist and poet, but William and Walter got on well. They became friends and although the simple, even frugal life of the Wordworths wasn't entirely to Scott's more refined tastes, he continued to visit them in the Lake District. The two men talked and walked, discussed ideas and read each other's work in progress.

Meanwhile, the third member of the original trio of romantic poets, Robert Southey, was also trying to earn a living writing. His friendship with Coleridge had been repaired, just. In the late summer of 1803, Robert and his wife Edith travelled up to Keswick to holiday with the Coleridges at Greta Hall. The visit also allowed Southey and Wordsworth to renew their acquaintance.

The plan was to stay just a couple of months. However, in December 1803, Coleridge, restless and unhappy, once more walked out on his wife and family. This obliged the gentlemanly Southey to remain at Greta Hall so that the two sisters, Edith and the abandoned Sara and her children, could be together. It also meant that there was added pressure on Southey to provide not just for his own growing family, eventually to swell to eight children (although two died in infancy), but Sara and her three children as well.

Sara Coleridge began to compare her husband's 'indolence' with Southey's hard work and caring attitude. Harriet Martineau would later comment 'that Southey worked double-tides to make up for Coleridge's idleness.' On the plus side, the Southey and Coleridge children, who were cousins, had each other as companions and playmates. Indeed, as they got older, the Greta Hall children also became regular visitors to Dove Cottage and Rydal Mount where they enjoyed the company of the Wordsworth family. In particular, the girls of all three poets became the best of friends.

Throughout these years of comings and goings, Humphry Davy remained friends with both Southey and Coleridge. He became a regular visitor to the Lake District, often staying with the Southeys at Greta Hall. It was during one of these visits that Davy finally met the Wordsworths.

In 1805, science and poetry united on a climb to the summit of Helvellyn. Wordsworth, Southey, Walter Scott and Humphry Davy walked and talked their way to the top of the mountain, each later to be affected and poetically inspired by the sad story of Charles Gough and his little dog, Foxie.

In late July 1805, a shepherd made a gruesome discovery beneath the eastern, precipitous slopes of Helvellyn. He heard a dog barking by the rocks on the shores of Red Tarn. She led him to a headless corpse and a pile of bleached bones. The shepherd found a notebook among the fraying clothes which revealed that the unfortunate body was that of Charles Gough, a young artist from Manchester. On 17 April he had set off on a walk to Grasmere along Striding Edge. It seems that as he was approaching the summit of Helvellyn he must have slipped and fallen to his death.

The discovery caused a local sensation. However, it was the dog's apparent loyalty that tugged at the heartstrings. The story appealed to Wordsworth who wrote a poem, 'Fidelity', to honour the dutiful dog staying by her master's side. Walter Scott, too, wrote a poem, 'Helvellyn', based on the faithful little dog. The tragedy clearly appealed to the Romantic vision.

Not only were poems written about the martyred artist but painters too had a go at rendering the tearful scene. Wild, indifferent nature was contrasted with man's quest for beauty and the little dog's loyal spirit.

In his painting titled *Attachment*, Edward Landseer imagined Gough lying on his back, dead, wrapped in a brown cloak, his left arm dangling over a rocky outcrop. Above the sheer cliffs looms a dark, brooding sky. With her paws resting on her master's chest, little Foxie is looking mournfully into the closed eyes of the dead man. In contrast to Landseer's picture of pathos, Francis Danby painted an altogether wilder scene of menacing mountains and wild winds which he titled *The Precipice*. Gough's body is splayed across a jagged ledge. His arms are flung to either side in the manner of a crucifixion. Strangely clad in what appears to be little more than a loin cloth, Gough is attended by his dog who is looking up towards a tormented skyline.

But of course, the dog's survival as she lay by the corpse, stripped of all flesh in less than three months, begged the question, what did she eat? Dog-lovers said little Foxie ate grass.

Coleridge returned to Greta Hall again in October 1806, by now hopelessly addicted to the drug laudanum – opium dissolved in alcohol. It was during this stay that he announced his intention to separate from Sara and his children, though this final parting didn't actually take place until 1812 when he made his last visit to the Lake District. Coleridge's abandonment of his wife and children at Greta Hall decided Southey that he would remain in Keswick. The friendship between Southey and Coleridge never really survived this wanton neglect of wife and children. Southey remained at the Hall for the rest of his life.

* * *

Living back in the Lakes had a profound effect on Wordsworth's poetry, in which the natural landscape and the rhythms of the year featured more and more. The lives of ordinary, everyday people – farmers, shepherds, local schoolmasters – became the subject of many of his poems. 'Common speech' was preferred to the high flown and high blown verses of eighteenth-century poets. In 'Ode: Intimations of Immortality from Recollections of Early Childhood', Wordsworth sums up his philosophy in the final four lines:

> Thanks to the human heart by which we live,
> Thanks to its tenderness, its joys, and fears,
> To me the meanest flower that blows can give
> Thoughts that do often lie too deep for tears.

During one of their walks in April 1802, William and Dorothy visited Gowbarrow Park on the northern shores of Ullswater, about halfway between Pooley Bridge and Glenridding. They couldn't help but notice the profusion of wild daffodils, smaller and paler that the cultivated varieties so common today. Dorothy's presence, descriptions and beautifully crafted journal notes played a key part in Wordsworth's development of what is perhaps his best known and probably best loved poem, 'I Wandered Lonely as a Cloud'. Although we know that William always read Dorothy's writings, he rarely acknowledged his debt. Take for example the following entry from her *Grasmere Journal*, dated 15 April 1802:

> I never saw daffodils so beautiful they grew among the mossy stones about & about them, some rested their heads upon these stones as on a pillow for weariness & the rest tossed & reeled & danced & seemed as if they verily laughed with the wind that blew upon them over the Lake, they looked so gay ever glancing and changing.

Mary too contributed, suggesting a couple of lines that her husband thought were the best two of the whole poem:

> They flash upon the inward eye
> Which is the bliss of solitude.

I know I shouldn't, because everyone does, but I can't resist quoting the opening lines of the poem if for no other reason than, like millions of young school children over the decades, it was one of the first poems I ever learned. Even as I'm about to write the words, I'm back at Heyes Lane Primary School in Timperley, sometime in 1956, along with my fifty-four classmates (yes, fifty-four, plus me) reciting:

> I wandered lonely as a cloud
> That floats on high o'er vales and hills,
> When all at once I saw a crowd,

A host, of golden daffodils,

Beside the lake, beneath the trees,

Fluttering and dancing in the breeze.

As the poems flowed, the Wordsworth family grew. Firstborn John was followed by Dora (1804), Thomas (1806), Catherine (1808), and finally William (1810). Mary's sister, Sara, the unrequited love of Coleridge's life, often looked after the Wordsworth children as well as helped copy many of the poems written by both Wordsworth and the lovelorn Coleridge.

With his growing fame, Wordsworth also attracted an increasing number of distinguished visitors. For example, in 1806 John Constable was on a sketching trip to the Lakes. He produced a number of pencil and wash pictures of the hills and clouds in various moods which gave him the idea of paying a visit to see William. The two men met, possibly at Brathay Hall. Constable outlined a quick portrait of the poet which has only recently come to light having been stored in the Royal Albert Memorial Museum in Exeter.

The Dove Cottage years were probably the most creative for William. In 1802, the *Edinburgh Review* wrote a rather dismissive piece about Wordsworth, Coleridge and Southey. The article lumped them all together, and in an attempt to belittle and diminish their efforts it dubbed them 'the Lake Poets', although it would be another year before Southey found himself living in the Lake District, while Coleridge had actually had his *annus mirabilis* in 1797 when he was living in the south-west. But the name stuck.

* * *

The Wordsworths eventually outgrew the tiny Dove Cottage. In 1808 the family moved to Allan Bank, a larger house on the north-western fringes of Grasmere. Thomas De Quincey, who had long been a fan of both Wordsworth and Coleridge, took on the rental of Dove Cottage and lived there for the next ten years.

He was born in Manchester on 15 August 1785. Seen as a very bright boy he eventually found his way to the University of Oxford, but of course, like so many of the Lakeland writers, he failed to take his final degree. And like his hero Coleridge, he also began taking opium.

De Quincey was a prolific writer, though not all that he drafted was published. Today he is best remembered for his autobiography *Confessions of an English Opium-Eater*, published in 1821. The ostensible aim of the book was to warn the reader of the dangers of opium use, but there are many passages where he writes about the wonderful effects the drug had on him.

> Oh! just, subtle, and mighty opium! that to the hearts of poor and rich alike, for the wounds that will never heal, and for 'the pangs that tempt the spirit to rebel' bringest an assuaging balm; eloquent opium! that with thy potent rhetoric stealest away the purposes of wrath; and to the guilty man, for one night givest back the hopes of his youth, and hands washed pure of blood ...

Not exactly a turn-off then, anticipating, as it does, many other drug-inspired 'addiction' novels and short stories over the last couple of centuries. Of course, prefiguring them all is Coleridge himself, especially in his poem 'Kubla Khan', which he described as a 'psychological curiosity'. It was probably inspired while he was staying in North Devon and was under the influence of opium. It's a poem about many things, including creativity, drug-induced dreams and pleasure. Here are the poem's famous opening first few lines:

In Xanadu did Kubla Khan
A stately pleasure-dome decree:
Where Alph, the sacred river, ran
Through cavern measureless to man
Down to a sunless sea.
So twice five miles of fertile ground
With walls and towers girdled round:
And here were gardens bright with sinuous rills
Where blossomed many an incense-bearing tree;
And here were forests ancient as the hills,
Enfolding sunny spots of greenery.

De Quincey's other autobiographical writings included *Lake Reminiscences,* first published in instalments in *Tait's Magazine* between 1834 and 1840. Although he purported to be a great friend and admirer of Wordsworth and his sister, at times his reminiscences could be rather malicious, even a little snobbish. He wrote that Dorothy had 'no personal charms'. He observed that William used a knife still smeared with butter to split open the pages of a brand-new book. The gossipy and candid accounts of the Lake Poets certainly helped boost the magazine's sales.

Having read the articles, Southey said De Quincey was a 'base betrayer of the hospitable social hearth'. De Quincey's biographer, Frances Wilson, recognising a clever, complex character, concluded that the self-titled 'Pope of Opium' was 'a fearless ironist' who united 'playfulness, venom, ambition, revenge and self-perception'. Perhaps reflecting this torn mix, one of De Quincey's more notorious essays, not to say successful, was titled 'On Murder Considered as One of the Fine Arts' (1827). De Quincey married and had eight children before his wife, Margaret, died in 1837. It would be another twenty-two, often troubled, years before his own death in 1859.

Chapter 7

FRIENDS, FAMILY AND FAME

Not long after the Wordsworths had moved to Allan Bank in 1808, Coleridge came to stay. This gave him the opportunity to visit his wife Sara and the children at Greta Hall. It also meant that he would be in daily company with Sara Hutchinson.

However, the relationship with the one-time love of his life was in slow decline. In the past Sara Hutchinson had accompanied Coleridge on some of his walks across the fells, acted as his secretary and even nursed him when he was ill. But she began to find his infatuation and the intensity of his feelings more and more oppressive. Her failure to wean him off his opium addiction was the final straw and led to their eventual estrangement in 1812.

The relationship between Coleridge and Wordsworth was also beginning to fray. The 1808 visit to Allan Bank was not a success although it dragged on for over a year. Coleridge's addiction to opium was as strong as ever. He would spend half the day in bed and was writing very little. Professional differences and arguments between the two men also grew. They ventured criticisms of each other's poetry, language and style. Coleridge valued the part that imagination played in the creative act. Wordsworth based his works on the everyday and the natural. However, it was Coleridge's lifestyle, indolence and dependence on laudanum that was really beginning to irritate Wordsworth. Their friendship suffered badly. It was something of a relief when Coleridge finally decided to take up the offer of a lift with Basil Montagu and to stay with him in London.

And so Coleridge headed south to London. In 1810, rumour and gossip that Wordsworth had warned Montagu that he would find Coleridge a difficult, self-absorbed guest eventually reached Coleridge himself. Like all gossip, things got exaggerated in the telling. Wordsworth's alleged descriptions of Coleridge as a drunkard and a mighty nuisance upset him considerably. Inevitably this soured relationships between the two poets even further. Their once great friendship never fully recovered from the rupture, although Wordsworth did attempt some repair work when he visited London in May 1812. The reconciliation was partially successful and the two men did see each other from time to time, but the heady days of their high energy, magnificently creative relationship were over.

Initially, Coleridge tried to ease the loss of both Wordsworth and Sara Hutchinson with more alcohol. His life descended into one of despair, depression and ill health, not helped by the heavy drinking and his continued addiction to opium. However, he did manage to write some poetry, and beginning in the autumn of 1811 he delivered a series of brilliant lectures on Shakespeare and Milton.

This was also the year in which the Wordsworths once more uprooted, moving to the parsonage in Grasmere. Then, less than two years later, they made their final move. In May 1813, they left Grasmere to settle a couple of miles down the road in their new, rented home, Rydal Mount, just north of Ambleside. Their year or so at the parsonage had been a difficult, if not to say traumatic, one. Two of William and Mary's children died. Catherine died not long before her fourth birthday. And six months later, after a bout of pneumonia, her older brother, Thomas died aged only six. The Wordsworths were grief-stricken.

Rydal Mount was originally a sixteenth-century farm cottage but additions and improvements eventually turned it into a 'gentleman's residence'. The house lies at the end of a short, rising road off what is now the A591 at Rydal. As it passes by Rydal Mount, the road trails off into a path that takes you to Heron Pike and the beginnings of that most satisfying of fell walks, the round that is the Fairfield Horseshoe.

* * *

As today, so then, poets generally didn't earn a lot of money, especially in their early years. Robert Southey was ferociously busy writing his biographies, essays, reviews and poems. He began to enjoy increasing success, especially as a critic for the *Quarterly Review*, however, few of Southey's poems, perhaps with the exceptions of 'Inchcape Rock' and 'After Blenheim', are remembered or read much today. His biographical writing has fared better. *The Life of Nelson* (1813) and *The Life of Wesley; and the rise and progress of Methodism* (1820) are still regarded as classics. National recognition came in 1813 when, at the relatively young age of thirty-nine, Robert Southey became poet laureate, a post he held for the next thirty years. At last his energy and hard-work began to earn him a good income.

He had arrived in the Lakes as a passing visitor but ended up spending the rest of his life there. However, Southey never developed that intimate relationship that Wordsworth had with the rivers, lakes and mountains. His success and recognition also coincided with his intellectual journey from left to right. By the time he died, his journey from young utopian radical to old Tory conservative was complete.

Wordsworth, though, needed money over and above the royalties generated by his writings. In the same year that Southey became poet laureate, William accepted the grandly titled post of Distributor of Stamps for Westmorland, Whitehaven and the Penrith Area of Cumberland. It was his first proper paid job; he was forty-three. The stamps in question were not mere postage stamps. They were sheets of stamped paper, issued by the Treasury, and legal documents were written on them. So to all intents and purposes Wordsworth became a government tax collector. But the job and its income did give him time and space to write.

By now the Wordsworths and Southeys were very much part of local life. On the night of 21 August 1815, a huge bonfire was lit on top of Skiddaw to celebrate the victory at Waterloo. Southey organised the event. And along with his family and many others from Keswick and the surrounding villages, he was joined by William, Mary, Dorothy, and ten-year-old Jonny. Beef was roasted on the fire. Plum puddings were boiled. Hot rum punch was drunk. And there was singing and dancing through the small hours into the next morning.

As Wordsworth's fame grew, more and more people made their way to Rydal Mount to pay the great man a visit, or simply to peer into his garden hoping to get a view of the aging poet. On 27 June 1818, with no appointment, the young poet John Keats called at the Mount – everyone was out, so he left a note.

Meanwhile, down in Highgate village, just north of London, Coleridge agreed to become a house patient of James Gillman, a young surgeon. The hope was that the good doctor would help him overcome his various addictions. He first moved in with the Gillmans in 1816, planning to stay a month. In the event he remained with them for the rest of his life. He failed in his attempts to give up alcohol and drugs. His hair had turned white. His aches and pains remained. Nevertheless, his wit and conversational virtuosity could still dazzle visitors.

In his writings, he continued to urge readers to let their imaginations run free, famously writing that to enjoy literature there had to be 'a willing suspension of disbelief'. His poetry, especially 'The Rime of the Ancient Mariner', 'Kubla Kahn' and 'Christabel', finally published together the year he moved in with Gillman, still had a strong fan base and he received many visitors, among them John Stuart Mill, James Fenimore Cooper, Ralph Waldo Emerson, Walter Scott and Thomas Carlyle – quite an intellectual line-up.

In April 1823, his wife and their bright, beautiful twenty-year-old daughter, also named Sara, visited Coleridge in Highgate. Ten years had passed since he had last seen them. That same month, William, Mary and Dorothy Wordsworth, along with Sara Hutchinson, dined with Coleridge and other guests.

Although he was greatly saddened by his ruptures with Wordsworth and Sara Hutchinson, with age and the passage of time, the visit allowed some healing to take place and further reconciliation to be achieved. In 1828, Coleridge, Wordsworth and Wordsworth's daughter, Dora, travelled together on a two-month tour of Europe. But Coleridge's health continued to deteriorate. For half of his life he had been predicting his own death, wracked as he was by rheumatism, constipation, aches and pains, all of which he self-medicated with laudanum, but which actually made many of his symptoms worse. He was anticipating his death and final release when he wrote his own epitaph in 1833, part of which reads:

> That he who many a year with toil of breath
> Found death in life, may here find life in death!

Samuel Taylor Coleridge died on 25 July 1834, aged sixty-one, of heart and lung problems and the years of damage caused by his opium addiction. He is buried in the aisle of St Michael's Church in Highgate.

Wordsworth, still walking and gardening, remained fit and healthy. His manner was quiet, even taciturn. His face became craggy and weather-beaten, matching the landscape about which he continued to write. His deep voice never lost its Cumberland accent.

At last, honours began to come his way. In 1838 the University of Durham awarded him an honorary doctorate in civil law. The public oration was delivered in English and not, as William expected, Latin. The poet, perhaps a little snootily, was not impressed, ironic perhaps as he had spent a literary lifetime championing plain speaking and down-to-earth writing.

However, the following year, the University of Oxford put matters right. Wordsworth received another honorary doctoral degree, again in civil law, and this time the oration, given by the Reverend John Keble, *was* in Latin. Keble said that Wordsworth was unique among poets 'because he alone had placed the customs, pursuits and moral observances of the poor not just in a good light, but even a heavenly one'. In her excellent biography of Wordsworth, Juliet Barker adds her own thoughts:

> Keble's oration gave the highest possible sanction to this interpretation, which could once have been regarded as blasphemous. It endorsed the crucial shift in critical and popular opinion, which now recognised as William's greatest strengths what had been once seen as his weaknesses. He had succeeded in educating a whole new generation to believe that Cumberland beggars and daffodils were fit subjects for poetry, that philosophical truths could be found in humble subjects and that religion could and should rise above sectarian differences.

Robert Southey's wife, Edith, died in 1837. For a while he had been corresponding with another poet, Caroline Bowles. Clearly they had more than poetry in common, and two years after Edith's death, in June 1839, Robert married Caroline. But less than four years later, on 21 March 1843, after rapidly deteriorating physical and mental health, Southey himself died and was buried in the churchyard of St Kentigern's at Great Crosthwaite, Keswick. He had been poet laureate for thirty years. The vacant post was offered to Wordsworth. Initially feeling that he was too old, Wordsworth finally accepted the honour just a few days before his seventy-third birthday.

He lived seven more years, dying of pleurisy on 23 April 1850, aged eighty. Three years earlier, his beloved daughter Dora had predeceased him. She was buried in the churchyard of St Oswald's, Grasmere. Wordsworth asked that he be buried alongside her.

Wordsworth had carried on writing to the very end, like Southey, his radical youth left far behind. As old age approached, he moved from republican idealist to Tory-supporting, Established Church worshipper. But his romantic roots never left him. His belief that the love of nature leads to the love of our fellow men and women was ever present in his poetry. If his overt politics were less radical, his ecological passions remained as strong as ever. If ecology is concerned with the interconnectedness of all things and the complex relationship between plants and animals, rocks and rain, then Wordsworth's belief that man and nature are intimately related reveal him as a man with deep ecological sensibilities. In this sense, he remained radical all his life, with roots growing ever deeper into the Cumbrian soil.

As Jonathan Bate notes, Wordsworth's 'love of nature' anticipated the idea of an 'environmental consciousness'. Environmental green remained his true colour, even as he drifted politically from red to blue. Bate sees the ecological sympathies of Wordsworth's later years as a continuation of the more overt political radicalism of his youth. In the late eighteenth and early nineteenth centuries, 'Scientists,' wrote Jonathan Bate in his 1991 book *Romantic Ecology*:

made it their business to describe the intimate economy of nature; Romantics made it theirs to teach human beings how to live as part of it ... the Romantic ecology has nothing to do with flight from the material world, from history and society – it is in fact an attempt to enable mankind the better to live in the material world by entering into harmony with the environment.

One of the last pieces Wordsworth was working on was his vast autobiographical poem. He had been composing the piece, off and on, for many years. He gave the blank verse the working title 'Poem to Coleridge'. After his death, William's wife, Mary, tidied matters up and sent the poem off to the publishers, retitling it 'The Prelude, or Growth of the Poet's Mind'.

It is a vast autobiographical poem covering his childhood, schooldays and his increasingly sharpened sensibilities and mystical experiences with nature. In contemplating a rock or a rill, a shepherd or a sky, the poet's mind is at the same time reflecting back on itself, exploring the relationship between the object of contemplation and the mystery of the subjective mind in the act of contemplating. In the process the very nature of self is being explored.

Many now regard 'The Prelude' as his greatest work, but tackling it is not for the faint hearted. In 2010, the Faculty of English at his old University of Cambridge took on the challenge of reading out loud the whole poem. It took the thirteen professors and faculty members ten hours to recite it in full.

Stepping back, in her biography of Wordsworth, Julia Barker quotes Stanton Biggs, an obituary writer for *Soulby's Ulverston Advertiser*, who writing for the 25 April 1850 edition, said:

It would be almost impossible to exaggerate or over-estimate the importance of the influence which Wordsworth, in conjunction with Coleridge, has exercised in the formation of the intellectual characteristics of the present age. These two alone have effected a complete revolution in our modes of thought and of expression ... the whole of the poetry that has issued from the English press for years has been tinctured and coloured by the genius of Wordsworth.

Sister Dorothy died on 25 January 1855, aged eighty-three years. She remained William's close companion and literary support all her life, continuing to live with her brother even after his marriage. Dorothy's exquisite journals describe her walks and talks with William, the meetings they had with Coleridge and Southey, Walter Scott and Charles Lamb, and her own reflections on what they saw and said as they wandered by the lakes and over the fells.

For much of her later life, Dorothy was unwell, often taking to her bed. With advancing age, she slowly began to lose her mind. Her heightened sensitivities, emotional intensity and easily aroused sensibilities had always been in marked contrast to those of both her brother and sister-in-law's more reserved characters. However, in spite of her delicate temperament and increasing invalidities, both mental and physical, Dorothy outlived William.

Mary Wordsworth, née Hutchinson – steady, calm and unflustered to the end – died on 17 January 1859 aged eighty-eight. She died, as she had lived, contented with her lot. Before her death she had requested that room be made for her in the overcrowded corner of Grasmere's churchyard where the Wordsworths were buried. Her request was granted. The grave was deepened and her coffin eventually was laid to rest by those of William and their beloved daughter Dora, surrounded by the yew trees that Wordsworth himself had advised some years earlier to be planted in the churchyard.

The weathered tombstones now stare blindly towards Lord Crag and Heron Pike, through the trees and by the wall beneath which the River Rothay, tumbles and chatters. The river twists and turns through Grasmere village before flowing out into Grasmere itself. It reappears as it leaves the mere, cascading chatteringly white over the low, little weir, babbling through the woods beneath White Moss Common before once more relaxing as it eases into Rydal Water.

The last leg of the River Rothay's short, busy journey takes it close by Rydal Mount, past Fox How, through the western fringes of Ambleside, by the roman fort of Galava, before finally slackening and slipping quietly and disappearing into Windermere's northern reaches.

Chapter 8

LAKES

Windermere is England's largest lake. It is nearly six square miles in area, though never very wide. It is known as a ribbon lake, running north–south for just over eleven miles. When the glaciers retreated towards the end of the last Ice Age around 10,000 years ago, the gouged valleys they left behind filled with the ice sheet's melting waters to form the lakes we know today.

Windermere, then, is Cumbria's largest lake, after which there are dozens and dozens of flashes of water, gradually diminishing in size from lakes to tarns to pools to puddles. However, there is general agreement that there are sixteen decent-sized lakes in the Lake District, and here they are, in descending size, courtesy of the Lake District National Park:

> Windermere – 14.8 square kilometres
> Ullswater – 8.9 square kilometres
> Derwent Water – 5.5 square kilometres
> Bassenthwaite Lake – 5.3 square kilometres
> Coniston Water – 4.0 square kilometres
> Haweswater – 3.9 square kilometres
> Thirlmere – 3.3 square kilometres
> Ennerdale Water – 3 square kilometres
> Wastwater – 2.9 square kilometres
> Crummock Water – 2.5 square kilometres

Esthwaite Water – 1 square kilometre
Buttermere – 0.9 square kilometres
Grasmere – 0.6 square kilometres
Loweswater – 0.6 square kilometres
Rydal Water – 0.3 square kilometres
Brotherswater – 0.2 square kilometres

None of them is very big by international standards, but there are lots of them, in a relatively small area, and they're all beautiful. And then of course there are the tarns, *tarn* being the Norse word for pool. A few of the bigger tarns, such as Seathwaite Tarn and Grisedale Tarn, are not much smaller than the smaller lakes.

This is the moment we need to get pedantic. As all pub quizzers know, there is only one lake in the Lake District: Bassenthwaite Lake. Mere is the Old English for lake, and Water of course means stretch of water or lake. So to call Windermere 'Lake Windermere' is tautological – Lake Winder-Lake. Other than Bassenthwaite, lake is built into the nomenclature of the remaining non-lake lakes. But in practice we should be relaxed about language, certainly if you're arranging to meet someone in the middle of Windermere, the town.

The first person to swim Windermere's full length of eleven and a bit miles was Joseph Foster in 1911. Today there are regular races and challenges to swim the length of the lake, and many completing the long, cold, sometimes choppy distance in under five hours. There are also races across the lake and by the lake, in summer and in winter. There are even events that involve swimming the lake both ways.

I first came across the Big Chill Swim in 2015. I think it was early February. The skies were leaden grey. The water temperature was around 8° C. The event was taking place, as it always did, in the Low Wood Bay marina on the north-eastern shores of

Windermere. There were hundreds of people, young and old, men and women, most in their bathing costumes. Wetsuits, of course, are for wimps, and were strictly not allowed. There were short thirty-metre dashes. There were relay races. And for the really hardy, a one-kilometre race. In February. Brrr. It was lovely to watch though, and quite inspirational. Well, perhaps not that inspirational. I stood, impressed, delighted, but steadfastly wearing my thermally lined, padded jacket and hat.

The lake has also been a tempting place for other brave, adrenalin-fuelled souls to satisfy their need for speed. On 13 June 1930, Sir Henry Segrave, already a holder of the land speed record, piloted his boat, *Miss England II*, to a new world water speed record of 98.76mph over two runs of Windermere. On his third run, the boat crashed at great speed killing both Segrave and his co-pilot Victor Halliwell.

Throughout much of the middle twentieth century there was great competition between the Americans and British to gain and regain the water speed record. For a while, Coniston Water became the preferred lake of the British on which to attempt the record. Malcolm Campbell drove and wrote about fast cars. He broke various land speed records, finally achieving the astonishing speed of over 301mph over two passes on the Bonneville Salt Flats in Utah on 3 September 1935. However, not content with driving very fast over land, he also wanted to move with speed across water. His boat was named *Blue Bird K4*. He set a series of records, his final one on Coniston Water. On the 19 August 1939, Sir Malcolm reached a speed of 141.74mph. Unlike many of his fellow record breakers, he died, aged sixty-three years, of natural causes.

Fate was less kind to his son, Donald Campbell. Donald took up his father's mantle. On 14 May 1959, his speed on Coniston Water reached a record breaking 260.35mph. In 1964 he became the first person to hold both the land and water speed records in the same year. Two years later, he set out to go even faster. And again, following in his father's footsteps, he took his boat, *Bluebird K7*, for trials on Coniston Water. It was late December 1966. The boat was powered by... a jet engine.

The team experienced a variety of mechanical problems and difficulties with the weather. But finally, on 4 January 1967, the boat was in good shape and the conditions on the lake were judged favourable. The average speed for the first run was 297.6mph. On the second run, *Bluebird* was reaching speeds of well over 300mph but before completing the required measured distance, the boat rapidly began to decelerate before flipping, still at great speed, into a cartwheel across the water. The boat broke apart under the severe impact killing Donald.

Although some of the wreckage was recovered over the following days, Donald Campbell's body was not found. It was not until 2000 that a determined effort was made to recover the bulk of the boat and once more, look for the body. The hull was raised from the lake bottom on 8 March 2001. It was not until 28 May of that year that Donald Campbell's body, but not his head, was finally found. He was still wearing his blue nylon overalls. He is buried in Coniston Cemetery where his grey slate memorial is brightened by the carved image of a vibrant blue bird.

The recovery and subsequent restoration of *Bluebird* by a group of Tyneside volunteers has, according to the lead engineer Bill Smith been a 'labour of love'. On Saturday 4 August 2018, the beautifully rebuilt craft was inched gently onto the waters of Loch Fad on the Isle of Bute to undergo a series of tests and trials, before she returns to Coniston Water once more to run at speed.

* * *

On a drowsy, still summer's day, not long after I had visited the cemetery, I was wandering by the lakeside. My eye was drawn to the faintest curl of light grey smoke. Moving sedately across the water, as she always does, was the yacht *Gondola*. Campbell's *Bluebird K7* was powered by a jet engine. *Gondola* is driven by steam. *Bluebird* reached speeds of over 300mph. *Gondola* cruises quietly at a gentle 8mph.

Originally a Victorian steam-powered boat launched in 1859, the year that Mary Wordsworth died, Steam Yacht *Gondola* was built to ferry passengers up and down the lake. James Ramsden was a director of the Furness Railway Company. He had visited Venice and rather liked the look of some of the city's larger barges, known as *burchiello*. They were powered by oar or pulled by horses, but it was Ramsden's plan to build a 'gondola', sail it on Coniston Water, and have it driven by steam. He was a railway man and knew all about steam locomotion. The yacht was built in Liverpool, taken to Coniston Water in sections, and assembled by the lakeside before her launch.

The steam yacht was in service right up until 1936. She is credited with giving Arthur Ransome his idea for Captain Flint's houseboat in his children's book *Swallows and Amazons*. After a brief, undignified spell as an actual houseboat, *Gondola* fell into disrepair and became derelict. Then, in the 1970s, the idea of trying to restore her was raised. With support and direction from The National Trust, money was found to return the boat to her former glory. Surveys revealed that a huge amount of work, replacement and rebuild would be necessary, but the yacht's supporters were undaunted. In the end it was the world-famous Vickers Shipbuilding and Engineering (now part of BAE Systems) of Barrow-in-Furness who agreed to take on the restoration.

Eventually all the pieces – hull, steam engine, boiler – were brought to the slipway at Piers Cottage by the jetty on Coniston to be put together. The choice of Piers Cottage was poignant, as it was where the boat was originally launched in 1859. The cottage was the home of one of the yacht's early masters, Captain Felix Hamill. He was captain from 1871 to 1913, a remarkable forty-two years of service. Piers Cottage was also Donald Campbell's base for his fatal attempt at the world water speed record. And so it was that on 25 March 1980, the exquisitely restored, beautifully fitted Steam Yacht *Gondola* was launched – by Sheila Howell, the great-granddaughter of Felix Hamill.

In these environmentally aware times, the steamship now burns logs of compressed sawdust instead of coal. But throughout the summer months, courtesy of her owner, the National Trust, she still takes passengers up and down Coniston Water, while the Old Man of Coniston looks on, casting his ancient gaze, as he has done throughout the ages, at humanity's comings and goings, hubris and folly, holidaying and heroism.

Gondola is the only true steamship still to sail the Lakes. The other lakes do have boats cruising up and down which the operators call 'steamers', but they are all powered by diesel. They are handsome ladies nevertheless. Windermere Lake Cruises runs a fleet of boats ranging in size from traditional launches up to the larger 'steamers'. They all have pretty names such as *Princess of the Lake*, *Miss Lakeland* and *Swan*. The Keswick Launch Company operates a busy timetable of cruises around Derwent Water, with seven landing stages en route for those keen to hop off and walk the hills.

And finally, Ullswater 'Steamers' sail five lovely boats the length and breadth of Ullswater, surrounded by its majestic hills. In his *Guide to the Lakes*, Wordsworth felt that Ullswater offered 'the happiest combination of beauty and grandeur, which any of the Lakes affords.' The oldest of the Ullswater 'steamers' is the *Lady of the Lake*. Built near Glasgow originally as a steam-powered vessel, MY *Lady of the Lake* was transported in three sections before being assembled on the slipway at Waterside by Pooley Bridge. She was launched on 26 June 1877 and has been gracing the lake with her elegant lines ever since.

In 1936 her steam engine was ripped out and replaced with a diesel-powered unit. Twice in her long life *Lady of the Lake* sank – in 1881 and again in 1958 after a severe storm. Even more catastrophic was the fire in 1965 that swept through her ageing bones as she was resting on the slipway at Watergate. For the next fourteen years she remained out of service. Then, like others whose beauty hadn't diminished with age, she was restored – extensively. Her old diesel heart was replaced with a new engine, and she has been as good as new ever since. To sail her, gliding between towering heights of Helvellyn to the south-west and Place Fell to the south-east, is a delight.

* * *

As well as being the largest of the lakes, Windermere is probably the busiest. On the surface boats sail, yachts tack, canoes paddle, swimmers swim, and if the winters are very cold, ice skaters skate. One such winter was 1805. In January of that year, many of the lakes froze including Grasmere and so, on the 18th of that month, William, Mary, and Dorothy Wordsworth went skating.

William was particularly fond of ice skating, although Thomas De Quincey would later write, with some cruel exaggeration, that watching Wordsworth skate and fall was like witnessing 'a cow dancing a cotillion'.

Though recent winters have been mild and the lakes rarely freeze, in the past, particularly the nineteenth century, long, cold winters often meant the waters turned to ice, and people gathered to enjoy skating parties – on Windermere, Derwent Water, indeed all the major lakes. In the 1890s, the hotels in Bowness used to reopen in January especially to cater for the ice skaters. And if the ice was particularly solid and thick, the lakes became highways – shortcuts for wagoners hauling their timbers, stones and metals across the flat, frozen waters.

On YouTube there is some extraordinary film footage of an ice-bound Windermere, 'Windermere – The Big Freeze 1963', when the lake was frozen for a couple of months or more. The film shows hundreds of people, young and old alike, ice skating. Ice hockey matches took place. Children, way out in the middle of the lake, were slipping and sliding against the familiar backdrops of the snow covered Langdales, Wansfell Pike, the lakeside hotels and the temporarily pointless jetties. The Big Chill Swim would certainly have had to live up to its name back then, breaking the metre-thick ice even to dip a toe in the cold waters beneath.

* * *

The lakes abound with birds that paddle and swim, dive and fish. Canada geese, coots and cormorants can be spotted in winter and summer. Mallard ducks and mute swans, greyling geese and red-breasted mergansers are also permanent residents. Stand by any lakeside with a bag of bird-friendly grain and you will be immediately popular with ducks and swans alike, and the inevitable, less welcome dive-bombing gulls. Other birds are visitors escaping the cold winters of Scandinavia and eastern Europe. The relatively mild winters and flashes of fresh water of the Lakes attract great-crested grebes, goldeneyes, tufted ducks and pochards.

Things are going on beneath the ripples too. These water-filled glacial valleys can be surprisingly deep. Bassenthwaite Lake is relatively shallow at around 62 feet (19 metres). At their deepest Grasmere and Derwent Water plunge 70 feet or so (22 metres). In its southern basin, Windermere sinks to 138 feet (42 metres) but as you swim north, the waters beneath your tiring arms deepen to well over 200 feet (64 metres). Best not to think about that as you end your eleven-mile effort. Deepest of all, though, is Wastwater. It comes in at an impressive 250 feet (76 metres).

What is also interesting to note is that although the surface of Wastwater lies 200 feet (61 metres) *above* sea level, the bottom of the deepest part of the lake actually sits 50 feet (15 metres) *below* sea level. It's a reminder that long ago, when ice sheets froze the land and glaciers ground their slow, relentless way through the mountains, valleys were deeper and sea levels lower.

Another reminder of Cumbria's Ice Age past is the presence of fish that, if not actually trapped in the lakes as survivors of the Ice Age, nevertheless are close relatives. For example, the Windermere charr is a large, red-bellied type of Arctic charr. It is a member of the salmonoid species and thrives in cold, deep water lakes. Mention was first made of its presence in the lake in 1540. It is said to have a delicate, trout-like taste. But in recent years its numbers have declined. Blame has been put on falls in the levels of oxygen in the water, rising lake temperatures, increases in pollutants and lower water quality as fertilisers wash-off from surrounding fields and phosphorus is pumped out from treated sewage, made worse by a growing population around the lakeside boosted by ever-higher tourist numbers.

* * *

As all fell walkers, map readers and lake lovers know, most of the lakes, as Wordsworth observed, are linear and ribbon-like, radiating out from some central hub like the spokes of a wheel. The hub of this imaginary watery wheel centres somewhere around Dunmail Raise, deep in the heart of Cumbria, although personally

I think it all revolves around Great Castle How, a craggy rise above Easedale Tarn, a couple of miles south-east of Dunmail Raise. The radial pattern also reflects the roughly circular, dome-like topography of the Lake District, with many of the highest, most rugged fells rising up and around Grasmere Common – Helvellyn and Fairfield to the east, Great Gable and Scafell Pike to the west, and the Langdales and Crinkle Crags to the south. The next chapter looks at how this came about.

Chapter 9

AN OCEAN, ANCIENT AND DEEP

The climb up from the valley is steep but short. Hind Gill burbles to my left. An hour and a half or so later, after a final scramble, I am standing on top of Glaramara. It peaks at 2,569 feet or 783 metres. It rises in the Central Lakes between Seathwaite at the head of Borrowdale and Langstrath Beck to the east.

A few clouds are bubbling high above me and I have a good all-round view. Looking north along Borrowdale I can see Skiddaw. To the south I can make out the Langdale Pikes, Bow Fell and Scafell Pike. The dome of Great Gable swells to the west.

From here, I have a good sense of the lie of the land. The steady slopes and rounded tops of the Skiddaw ridge to the north contrast with the more raggedy, craggedy terrain that immediately surrounds me. And way to the south, but difficult to see from where I'm standing, is the more subdued, undulating scenery around Windermere.

In a rough and ready fashion, these three contrasting areas of upland map out the geology of the Lake District. And around this core of older, higher, harder, mountain rocks of the central Lakeland dome lies a broken ring of younger, lower, softer, mainly sedimentary rocks.

One of the first people to notice this sequence of rocks was the Keswick watchmaker Jonathan Otley. He was a gifted amateur scientist and an inveterate walker of the dales and climber of the fells.

In 1820, when he was fifty-five years old, he published the first scientific maps and accounts of the complex geology of the Lake District. He noticed that as the rock types changed, so did the landscape and scenery. He also correctly worked out the order in which the three major rock groups of the Lakes – Skiddaw Slates, Borrowdale Volcanics and Windermere Sedimentaries – were laid down. A remarkable achievement for the untrained amateur. In 1823 Otley published a guidebook for tourists, *A Descriptive Guide to the English Lakes*, in which he incorporated his findings on the geology of the area.

Jonathan Otley was born in Nook House near Loughrigg Tarn on 19 January 1766, the same year as John Dalton. The house, also known less prettily as Scroggs, lies tucked beneath the western slopes of Loughrigg Fell, quietly overlooking woods and fields. It was a place to which Otley retreated throughout his life for short breaks and holidays. In 1791 he settled in Keswick where he established himself as a watchmaker and clock repairer.

As well as geology, this remarkable man's scientific interests also included botany, meteorology, mineralogy and topography. He acted as a scientific counterweight to Lakeland's growing reputation as a place for poets, artists and those with a Romantic turn of mind. He became a close friend of John Dalton. They first met by accident on 6 July 1812 as they both happened to be climbing Skiddaw. Otley noticed Dalton carrying a barometer and, of course, this excited his professional interest. Like Dalton, Otley took daily readings of temperature, rainfall and air pressure. The two friends knew that air pressure dropped with altitude and so by taking careful barometer readings they were among the first people to estimate the heights of many of Lakeland's mountains.

It is not known quite how Otley, self-taught, became so knowledgeable about so many things. It is thought that the Robert Southey gave Jonathan access to his library at Greta Hall. At the beginning of the nineteenth century the population of Keswick was not much more than one thousand souls, so most people knew who was who.

A good deal of Otley's geological knowledge came from talking to those who mined the Lake District's lead, copper and silver ores. His genius was to piece together their local expertise and add it to his own wide-ranging observations to make sense of the whole geological landscape and the ancient rocks of Cumbria.

Throughout his long life, Jonathan Otley never lost his curiosity about the world around him. He observed the wind, measured the rain, mapped the rocks, studied the flowers. He died at his home in Keswick on 7 December 1856, aged ninety. There is a commemorative plaque for Otley on the wall of Kings Head Court in Keswick, near where for so many years he mended clocks and watches and made his instruments.

* * *

The famous pioneering geologist and one of the founding fathers of the discipline, Adam Sedgwick, professor of geology at Cambridge, regularly consulted Otley for his views on the geology of Cumbria. Although Sedgwick was twenty years younger than the Keswick man, the two of them often met up to walk, talk and try to make sense of the rocks, minerals and stratigraphy of Lakeland's hills and dales. Indeed, on one occasion in the summer of 1824, while Otley and Sedgwick were wandering over Armboth Fell above Thirlmere, before it became a reservoir, by chance they happened to bump into John Dalton. It's wonderful to picture these three great men of early nineteenth century science ambling down to the Nag's Head Inn at Wythburn, below Helvellyn, where they spent the evening together. Indeed, this coming together of so much talent becomes even more extraordinary when it is remembered that during his fieldtrips between 1822 and 1824, Sedgwick would sometimes stay with Robert Southey at Greta Hall as well as meet up and chat with Wordsworth.

Clearly benefitting from Otley's local knowledge, between 1831 and 1855 Sedgwick published a series of papers on the rocks of the Lake District and 'the general Structure of the Cumbrian Mountains'. William Wordsworth invited Sedgwick to write a few brief 'letters' on the geology of the area that he added to later editions of his *Guide to the Lakes*, of which we'll hear more about in Chapter 15.

I'm not sure how true it is today, but certainly the nine-teenth-century traveller appreciated a bit of geology being thrown into the text of any well-rounded guide to the Lake District. Sedgwick wanted 'to address more general readers – any intelligent traveller whose senses are open to the beauties of the country around him … and to point out the right way towards a compre-hension of some of its general truths.'

However, in spite of Wordsworth's recognition that a bit of sci-ence and a few geological facts would be good for sales, he still doubted that the men of science had much poetry in them as evi-denced in this extract from his poem 'The Excursion', albeit written before he knew Professor Sedgwick:

> He who with pocket-hammer smites the edge
> Of luckless rock or prominent stone, disguised
> In weather-stains or crusted o'er by Nature
> With her first growths, detaching by the stroke
> A chip or splinter – to resolve his doubts,
> And, with that ready answer satisfied,
> The substance classes by some barbarous name,
> And hurries on …

Some barbarous name? 'Amygdaloidal basalt', 'felsitic rhyo-lite', 'volcanic tuff', 'rhyodacite'. Say the names of these geological terms out loud. There's poetry there, William, surely! And a story half-a-billion years old.

As Jonathan Otley observed, rocks and their different types shape our land. Their origins, nature and history seep into the character and sensibilities of those who live on their surface, including poets and painters. The flatlands of the Fens, barely above sea level, offer big skies and wide horizons. The rolling hills of the chalklands make for good walking country and, in ancient times, easy trade routes. Those who walk the chalk ridges have clear views of places to go and how to get there. The breathtaking, remote wilderness of the North West Highlands of Scotland speak of vast aeons of time embedded in the underlying Lewisian gneisses. The resilient, no-nonsense, dour Millstone Grit, gives the Pennines its backbone and its folk their character. And the sublime beauty of Cumbria's lakes and mountains continues to inspire walkers and wonderers, philosophers and poets, the curious and courageous.

* * *

To begin to understand Lakeland's rocky foundations we need to go back a long, long way in time. As I stand on Glaramara, I try to get a sense of the geological timescales involved, but our all too brief lives make the imaginative leap impossible.

Half-a-billion years ago, what is now Lakeland was a shallow sea on the edge of an ancient continental fragment known as Avalonia. It lay about 30 degrees *south* of the equator. To the east lay the island continent of Baltica, which eventually became the bedrock of much of current day Scandinavia and the Baltic. This was a time before the various bits of the British Isles became welded into the land we know today – to add to the imaginative leap required, Northern

Ireland and Scotland were part of an entirely *different* ancient continent, named Laurentia. It lay a couple of thousand miles to the north of Avalonia, separated by an ocean.

Geologists have called this vast sea the Iapetus Ocean. Its ultimate destiny was to close and disappear, but the name is suggestive. Today, of course, the Atlantic Ocean separates the Laurentian Mountains of Canadian Quebec from Europe. In Greek mythology, the titan Atlas was condemned to hold up the sky for all time; he also gave his name to the Atlantic Ocean. The father of Atlas was the titan Iapetus. Hence, the Iapetus Ocean, it being a kind of precursor of the modern day Atlantic Ocean.

Avalonia itself was a fragment – a mini-continent – of the ancient supercontinent of Gondwana. Lapping the shores of Avalonia, and sometimes drowning it altogether, were the shallow sea edges of Iapetus. The rivers of Avalonia drained into the ocean bringing with them sands and silts, and into the deeper parts, oozes and muds. Over millions of years these sediments settled on the bed of the sinking sea floor. Thousands of metres of muds and silts accumulated. In the tropical waters above the seabed lived trilobites and shell fish, sponges and corals. Life then was aquatic; this was a time before land plants or animals.

However, this tropical, southern home of our proto-Lakeland was not set to last.

Chapter 10

VOLCANOES

It was about 475 million years ago that the early world of the Lake District changed dramatically. The deep ocean waters were on the point of giving way to a land of fire and violence.

The Iapetus Ocean was fast disappearing, as Avalonia and Baltica began to drift north and west to Laurentia. A slow-motion collision of continental proportions was beginning to take place, all driven by plate tectonics.

The Earth's surface is a restless place. Huge slabs of the crust appear to drift slowly across the earth's surface, constantly reconfiguring the continents and rearranging the geography of the planet. The deep interior of the Earth is a very hot place, partly heated by the slow decay of radioactive elements. Temperatures are hot enough to melt rocks, although the great pressures mean that rather than exist as free-flowing lavas, the molten rocks are stiff, viscous and plastic. Nevertheless, they can and do flow, very slowly, like tar in the sun.

Between the base of the relatively solid crust and the Earth's core is a layer thousands of miles thick, known as the mantle. The top of the mantle, just beneath the crust, has temperatures ranging between 500° C and a 1,000° C. However, the lower reaches of the mantle can exceed 4,000° C. This heat difference between top and bottom sets up mighty, slow-moving convection currents in the Earth's molten, plastic mantle. Hot mantle rocks slowly rise, cool and sink setting up great circular currents that creep and flow beneath the solid crust.

As the tops of these convection cells flow slowly beneath the planet's solid surface, they drag the major crustal plates along with them. When the rising currents of two adjacent cells reach the mantle surface, they fan out and flow in opposite directions. These *diverging* currents stretch the crustal plates above them, tearing them apart. Where the crust separates, great chasms and ridges develop. Rift valleys, new seas and wide oceans begin to open. Volcanoes also erupt along the line of separation as new lavas well up and spill out to fill the gap between the diverging plates. Today's Mid-Atlantic Ridge and the volcanic islands that bead its length, including Iceland, the Azores, and St Helena, offers a dramatic example.

When two convection cells *converge*, cool and descend, the plates riding above them collide and dive, causing the crust above to rise and buckle. This results in great mountain chains such as the Himalayas and the Andes. It can also cause earthquakes and create island arcs of volcanoes and lava, as we see today in Japan and Indonesia. And this is what was happening in the Lake District as Avalonia and Laurentia drifted closer and closer.

Sandwiched between the two advancing lands was the thin oceanic crust of Iapetus and the thousands of metres of muds and silts, which lay over the sea floor. The squeezed oceanic crustal plate of Iapetus had nowhere to go other than plunge into the mantle deep *beneath* Avalonia, in a process known as subduction. As they were pushed down, the oceanic muds, silts and sands were bulldozed, crumpled and compressed. Under the increasing heat and pressure, these muddy sediments slowly turned to hard rock, destined in the Lake District to form the beds of the Ordovician Skiddaw Group, including the Skiddaw Slates that make up Skiddaw itself.

And still the plates ploughed on. Around 460 million years ago, some of the oceanic crust of Iapetus was forced so deep beneath the Avalonian plate that it began to melt. The subducted oceanic crust and the very top of the mantle turned to molten magma. Trapped sea waters also helped lower the melting point of the heated rocks.

Above the subduction zone the continental crustal rocks continued to buckle and fracture. This allowed the hot, melting rocks beneath to find their way to the surface. As they rose the pressure dropped, and the viscous rocks turned into hot, free-flowing lavas. Their final escape at the surface witnessed the opening of huge faults, fissures, the eruption of volcanoes, and massive flows of lava, layer upon layer. If you were boating around these parts all those years ago, what you'd see along the shores and in the shallow shelf seas of Avalonia would be very active volcanoes and new island arcs.

Initially, the shallow-sided volcanoes, vents and fissures poured out fairly silica-poor, fluid, 'effusive' magmas such as basalt and andesite, typically black or grey in colour. These 'effusive' eruptions formed vast lava flows, often tens of metres thick, one on top of another. There would also be times when the volcanic vents spat out and fired lumps of cooling magma high into the sky before they fell into the shallow surrounding seas or splattered onto the lava-layered land in rough, pebbly heaps that would later be compressed into rocks known as tuffs and volcanic breccias.

Rocks which form from molten magma are called 'igneous' rocks. Geologists have named these particular igneous, free-flowing, effusive lavas the Ordovician Lower Borrowdale Volcanic Group. Over time, new lavas flowed over old lavas, building one thick layer on top of another. In between the flows, quieter times sometimes led to the accumulation of sedimentary material, perhaps deposited in the shallow seas or coastal lakes. These thin sedimentary beds can be seen separating the thick lava flows. In some parts of the Lake District, the total thickness of these predominantly andesitic lavas and occasional sediments exceeded well over two kilometres.

The fells around Borrowdale, as the name implies, are some of the best places to see these ancient lava flows and their associated volcanic activity. They make for rough, rugged terrain. More broadly, the rocks of the Lower Borrowdale Volcanic Group stretch in an arc from Ullswater in the east, over the northern reaches of Thirlmere, High Rigg and Castlerigg Fell by Derwent Water, before heading south-west over Kirk Fell, Birker Fell, and finally south towards Wastwater and Eskdale's Harter Fell.

* * *

As the Iapetus Ocean crust continued its descent beneath Avalonia, the character of the volcanic eruptions began to change. The molten rocks beneath the leading edge of the advancing Avalonian plate became richer in silica-forming rocks known as dacite and rhyolite. These rocks are generally paler and lighter in colour than the basalts and andesites. The higher content of silica makes the magmas of dacite and rhyolite less fluid. The magmas are stiffer and more viscous.

When these less runny magmas near the surface, they don't flow so easily out of their vents and fissures. Instead, vents become clogged with congealing magma. Volcanic plugs form. Beneath the plugs, pressure continues to build and build until there is a massive explosion, rather like Mount St Helen's, which erupted in the USA's Washington State in 1980 with devasting effect. The Mount St Helen's eruption threw rocks and dust tens of thousands of feet into the air. Huge, hot flows of pulverised rock and ash, magma and gases tore down the mountainside at terrifying speeds for tens of miles, wasting everything in their path.

These explosive types of eruption which release millions of tons of ash, 'bombs' of solidifying magma and gases are known as 'pyroclastic' eruptions. The rocks they form are very different to the relatively gentle lava flows of andesite that we saw in the earlier Lower Borrowdale Volcanic Group. And because the flows and deposits from these pyroclastic, explosive vents were laid down a few million years later on top of the older basaltic and andesite lavas, round about 445 million years ago, they have been named the Upper Borrowdale Volcanics of the Ordovician Period. They are made up of lava flows of dacite, rhyolite as well as andesite, along with rock types called 'tuffs' formed from the pyroclastic flows and bursts of ash, lava 'bombs' and the shattered fragments of the older rocks through which the exploding gases and magmas erupted.

Tuffs vary enormously in character. Some are made from fine volcanic ash. Others are composed of ash, blasted rock fragments and solidified globs of viscous magma. Pyroclastic rocks made up of even coarser fragments, typically embedded in a finer ash matrix, are described as volcanic breccias. Some of the volcanic ash rolled into the seas surrounding the volcanoes. Some spread across the lava-strewn landscapes beneath the fuming vents.

Today, many of these rocks weather beautifully. Pick up a water-worn, smooth-polished stone from any central mountain ghyll or look beneath your feet as you tread on one of the steps so kindly laid by the volunteers of Fix the Fells. The chances are you'll see shards of bright angular white clasts set in a pale yellow-green matrix of volcanic ash; or fragments of black, shattered lava in a collage of glistening pale pink tuffs.

Having erupted vast amounts of viscous magma, these violent volcanoes sometimes collapsed into the emptied chambers below forming 'calderas', many of which became sea-swamped or lake-filled hollows. There were times, therefore, in between the violent eruptions when sediments of mud, silt and sand were deposited in these caldera lakes, lagoons and the shallow seas around them.

Although these sedimentary rocks later were 'cooked' by the heat and pressure of mountain formation, they can still be found today as layers sandwiched between the pyroclastic rocks and volcanic breccias. Some of the finer cooked and compacted sediments were destined to become the Lake District's distinctive green slates, including those of Honister and Elterwater.

And throughout all this time of tremendous volcanic activity, there were also slips and slides, fractures and faults, earthquakes and tsunamis, further destabilising the piles of ash, the layers of solidified magma, and the muddy sediments of volcanic lakes and surrounding seas.

Then after millions of years of lavas pouring and volcanoes exploding, things began to calm down and the volcanic action moved south to areas that now form the rocks and mountains of Snowdonia, West Pembrokeshire and Leinster in southern Ireland. By the time they had ended their fiery days, the Borrowdale Volcanics left behind them thousands of metres of lavas, tuffs and pyroclastics which, although contorted, tilted and generally messed around by the vast passages of geological time, we stare at, walk over and write about today.

* * *

However, beneath ancient Lakeland's lava flooded, battered volcanic landscape, there was one final heated throw of the dice. By now the remaining molten rocks generated by the Iapetus oceanic crust as it continued its deep dive beneath the Avalonian landmass were rich in super-heated waters. These waters were also saturated with gases including chlorine and fluorine. These liquids and gases were super-hot, volatile, fluid and highly mobile. They were rich in metallic minerals containing copper, lead, silver, zinc and many other precious metals. As these super-heated rocky liquids forced their way along cracks and crannies, faults and fissures, and made their way to the surface, they cooled and solidified leaving veins of quartz rich in metallic minerals. Over 400 million years later, these mineralised veins would be discovered and then mined by an inventive new species, homo sapiens.

Ores of many different metals have been found and mined across the Lake District. Copper has been extracted commercially in Borrowdale, the Newlands Valley, the Caldbeck Fells and the hills west of Coniston. Queen Elizabeth I established the Society of Mines Royal to encourage more mining work. In his examination of the archives, author and historian W. G. Collingwood (whose grand-children Arthur Ransome taught to sail in their grandfather's boat, *Swallow II*) records that:

> On December 10th, 1564, an indenture was made by the Queen on one part, and Thomas Thurland and Daniel Hechstetter on the other, by which these two were empowered to search, dig, dry, roast, and melt all manner of mines and ores of gold, silver, copper, and quicksilver, in the counties of York, Lancaster, Cumberland, Westmorland, Cornwall, Devon, Gloucester, and Worcester, and in Wales. The Queen was to have one-tenth of the native gold and silver ...

Queen Elizabeth I also agreed that labourers from Germany could be brought over to mine the metals. Most of them decided to settle in and around Keswick. By 1567, many had married Cumbrian wives. The parish register of Crosthwaite Church, Keswick records 176 children born to German fathers between 1565 and 1584.

Brigham, now a suburb of Keswick, was the site of a copper smelter. The crushing hammers and bellows were powered by water wheels on the banks of the River Greta. During the 1560s,

Keswick become a thriving industrial town operating six furnaces. Huge quantities of charcoal were needed to fire and smelt the ore, necessitating the felling of large numbers of trees. Peat was also used along with coal mined at nearby Workington. As well as copper, small quantities of other metals could be smelted from the ores, including silver, zinc and manganese.

Lead mines too were opened in several places, with the most productive found at Greenside in the valley of the Glenridding Beck on the eastern slopes of Helvellyn. This mine was active throughout the nineteenth century and didn't finally cease production until 1959.

Wolfram, an ore of tungsten, was also found over a hundred years ago. Tungsten is a heavy metal. It has a density of 19.3 grams per cubic centimetre, making it almost as heavy as gold. It has the highest melting point of any element. Tungsten is one of the toughest materials found in nature, especially when combined with carbon to produce tungsten carbide. Wolfram was mined on the slopes of a tributary valley of the River Caldew as it tumbled east down the slopes of Carrock Fell. These wolfram mines were most productive during the First and Second World Wars as they played their part in the two war efforts. Tungsten is used in light bulb filaments and as a hardener in steel production.

In general though, the heydays of metal mining in the Lake District ran between the late sixteenth and the early eighteenth centuries. All that is left today are overgrown spoil heaps and sealed mine shafts. It was during her summer holidays of 1901 and 1903 that Beatrix Potter explored some of the abandoned mines in the Lingholm and Fawe Park slopes overlooking Derwent Water. She discovered several old mine shafts, some shut off by an old solid wooden door set into the hillside. Beatrix sketched two of these doors. One closed the entrance to Yewthwaite Mine. The other shut off the abandoned Castle Nook Mine at Castle Rock. The sketch of one of these doors would later become the door featured in the pictures of Mrs Tiggy-Winkle's cosy little kitchen.

Graphite was also found in veins or 'pipes' on the fells above Seathwaite in the 1550s. Graphite is a form of the element carbon which in the past was also known locally as 'wad', plumbago or black-lead, although as Jonathan Otley pointed out in his early nine-teenth century guide, the names are 'erroneous ... as lead forms no part of its composition'.

For a long time the wad had been used by farmers to mark their sheep. Artists and painters then discovered that it was good for making pencil drawings. Graphite's remarkable properties then led to its use as a rust-proofer, an aid to casting cannon balls, a glaze for pottery and, of course, as a key constituent in the manufac-ture of 'lead' pencils, which became the basis of the world-famous Cumberland pencil industry based in Keswick. A factory owned by George Rowney in 1798 was possibly the world's first pencil fac-tory, though records are lost and so the title tends to be given to the Cumberland Pencil Company which opened in 1832. It has under-gone several changes of name and ownership, but it continues to this day at its new site in Workington.

Much of Lakeland's mining and smelting industry has therefore been the result of super-heated, mineralised waters surging beneath the miles of Skiddaw Slates and Borrowdale Volcanics some time back in the late Ordovician and Early Silurian Periods, hundreds of millions years ago. It was the cooling of these hydrolysed waters between the cracks and fissures in which the veins of quartz, copper, silver and lead ores began to form, charging the rocks with their precious cargo.

* * *

Then around 440 or so million years ago, during the Silurian Period, things quietened down. Sea, wind and rain began to erode the uppermost surfaces of the Borrowdale lavas and pyroclastic flows. Over the next 50 million years, the land sank, major river basins formed and shallow seas returned. The rivers deposited muds, silts and sand onto the seabed, while above the limey remains of shell-fish and plankton rained down. Sands, gravels and silts accumulated in the river valleys. Over time, these deposits consolidated into a variety of sedimentary rock types, including limestones. These softer sedimentary rocks now run east to west across the southern Lakes, over Windermere and by Coniston. Geologists have named this third and final group of southern Central Lake District rocks, the Windermere Supergroup of the Silurian Period.

This outline of central Cumbria's geology inevitably simplifies a complex story, but the basics offer a rough guide to Lakeland's rocks and scenery. It was Jonathan Otley of Keswick who first recognised and mapped the area's three main rock groups and how they deter-mined today's landscape. It's as the rock types change from north to south, oldest to youngest, volcanics to sedimentary that the beauty of the lakes and fells shift from the sublime to the sensuous, the dra-matic to the domesticated.

And just in case you were wondering, towards the end of this mighty collision between Avalonia and Laurentia, England and Scotland were about to become joined, to be stitched together along the suture line of the old Iapetus Ocean, now closed forever.

Chapter 11

MOUNTAIN BUILDING

Although things appeared to be quietening down on the surface, deep below, the mantle was still churning away. Its convection currents continued to drag the continental plates of Avalonia, Laurentia and Baltica towards their final shunt. By around 425 million ago years the crust beneath the Iapetus Ocean had all been subducted beneath the converging plates while above the Avalonian crust was pushed aloft, compressed and contorted.

The sedimentary and volcanic rocks that had accumulated throughout the late Cambrian, Ordovician and early Silurian Periods (roughly 500 million to 425 million years ago), began to rise and crumple, forming a vast mountain chain running from what is now southern Ireland, through Wales, the Lake District and the Scottish Highlands and across to Scandinavia. This ancient mountain chain, probably as high as the Alps are today, has been named the Caledonides by geologists, after the Scottish Caledonian mountains.

The Scottish rocks of the Grampians, North West Highlands and North Highlands had all originally been laid down on the continent of Laurentia on the *opposite* side of the Iapetus Ocean to the Avalonian rocks of the Lake District. Thus, not only did the Caledonian Orogeny (from the two Greek words, *oros*, mountain, and *geneia*, creation, birth) give rise to a major mountain chain, it also united, *for the first time*, Scotland with England and Wales. The north and south of the country were fused together as the two ancient continents underwent their final collision.

As you stand high on top of the Lake District's highest peaks and gaze north across the Solway Firth to Dumfries and Galloway, it is odd, and slightly mind-blowing, to think that 480 million years ago you would be staring across the great Iapetus Ocean, with Scotland far over the horizon a thousand miles or more in the distance. Today, where the two ancient continents were wrought together during the Caledonian Orogeny, the line of the 'stitch' is known as the Iapetus Suture. It runs through southern Ireland, then just north of the Isle of Man, across the Irish Sea, through the Solway Firth, then more or less along the border between Scotland and England before finally heading into the North Sea towards Norway.

Mountain building doesn't just push thousands of metres and great layers of rock high into the air, it also forces down roots of continental crust deep into the upper mantle. Imagine pushing two slabs of thick, multi-layered pastry together. The layers would fold and crumple, slip and slide, both above and below the impact zone in the middle. Although rocks can and do 'flow' under heat and pressure, they are more obdurate than pastry so they also fracture and fault, both on a small and large scale. Nevertheless, the extreme heat and pressure experienced in the centre of mountain building zones does alter rocks, physically and chemically. This is the process known as 'metamorphosis' and the rocks forged are known as metamorphics.

Metamorphic rocks form the third major rock type after igneous and sedimentary. The most familiar metamorphic rocks in the Lake District are the Skiddaw Slates. These slates formed as the Ordovician mudstones and siltstones were heated and compressed under the great pressures experienced deep in the heart of the Caledonide mountains.

If the heat and pressure become even greater, the rocks at the base of the rising mountain chain can actually melt. In the case of the Lake District this resulted in the production of granitic magmas. They plumed upwards and intruded themselves into the overlying older Skiddaw Slates and Borrowdale Volcanic rocks.

Not being near the surface, these deep-seated 'plutons' of magma cooled very slowly. This gave them time to grow large crystals of feldspar and quartz, seen to great effect on so many public buildings which use granite as their facing stone and on kitchen work surfaces so easy to wipe clean. It is thought that most of the Lake District is underlain by a large 'batholith' of granite. However, millions of years of erosion mean that surface outcrops of these big-crystalled granites do occur at, for example, Skiddaw, Eskdale, Ennerdale and Shap with its distinctive crystals of big, beautiful, pink feldspar.

After a few tens of millions of years, the Caledonian Orogeny finally came to a halt, ending around 390 million years ago. The great mountain chain it had created was now open to the elements and ripe for erosion by wind and rain, frost and snow, sun and heat.

* * *

We now need to trip briskly over the next 400 million years to get us to the Lake District as it was just two and half million ago – the beginning of the last Ice Age and, geologically speaking, almost yesterday. The experts among you will wince as I condense these few hundred million years into a few paragraphs, but here goes.

As is the fate of all mountains, the mighty Caledonides gradually eroded down, lower and lower. This wearing away took place during the Devonian Period, beginning around 400 million years ago. Rivers carried away the weathered pebbles, sands and clays out into new seas and oceans. By the end of the Devonian, the Lake District had been weathered to a flat plain. And all the time, the Earth's tectonic plates shifted this way and that over the surface of the planet, taking the continents with them.

If we recall, the rocks of the Skiddaw group and the volcanics of the Borrowdales were laid down when the Lake District was lying around 30 degrees *south* of the equator, down in the southern hemisphere. Over the next 400 million years, the whole of the newly forged British Isles drifted slowly north – across the equator (350 million years ago), over the tropic of Cancer at 30 degrees north (about 250 million years ago) before finally ending up where it is today between latitudes 50 and 58 degrees north.

At the same time as the Lake District and the rest of the British Islands were carried north, the tectonic plates continued to bump and bustle over the planet, breaking up old continents and creating new ones, closing old oceans and opening up fresh seas. This combination of the drift north and the restless reconfiguration of the continents and oceans meant that both the climate and the topography of the Lake District were constantly changing. This also meant that the sediments, and their compaction and 'lithification' into various rock types also shifted in character. Each of these major developments defines the great geological periods.

As the Caledonian mountain chain began to be worn down and the Eurasian plate continued drifting north, the climate became hotter and drier. Britain was now part of a sandy, semi-arid landmass with vast river flood plains (the Devonian Period).

When the British Isles found themselves straddling the equator, the land became submerged under warm, coral rich seas and coastal lagoons in which thick beds of (Carboniferous) limestone were laid down. Further fluctuations of land and sea influenced the types of sediments rivers brought down from the Scottish-Scandinavian mountains. Muds, silts, sands and grits fanned out to fill the seas and form mighty deltas. Today these sediments are to be seen as the shales and coarse sandstones of the (Carboniferous) Millstone Grits.

The deltas gradually turned into a low-lying, warm, wet, swampy world. It supported a rich vegetation of tropical forests including giant ferns and horsetails. The deposits of silt, sand and decaying plant life became compressed to form the (Carboniferous) coal measures. Today, the Ordovician and Silurian rocks of the Lake District are encircled by these younger Carboniferous limestones, sands and coal measures, including the coals to be found and mined between Maryport and Whitehaven.

And still the British Isles continued their drift north. After the Carboniferous Period (359 to 299 million years ago), the region oscillated between being a place of rivers and land, shallow shelf seas, and deserts and salt flats. Each of these different regimes gave rise to different deposits and rock types, although few are to be found in the Lake District today.

Around 280 million years ago another phase of mountain building took place. This is known as the Variscan Orogeny. Most of the plate-colliding action took place to the south of the Lake District over middle Europe and across to Devon and Cornwall. However, the northern ripples of the Variscan crumple zone caused the rocks of the Lake District to buckle into a dome. The Carboniferous rocks pushed up in the middle of the dome were gradually worn away so that today we find none of them present in the central Lakes. They do, however, as we have seen, form a ring of younger rocks surrounding the older rocks of the Lake District's mountains. The limestone cliffs of Scout Scar just a mile or so west of Kendal offer a fine example of the geology of this period.

Following Carboniferous times, the hot dry conditions continued. Permian limestones, sea salts and sands were laid down and can now be found in long north–south outcrops running along the eastern side of the country, although there is a Permian strip running along the Eden valley east of Penrith.

By 250 million years ago, Britain was a place of deserts and sand dunes, shallow lakes and salty waters. This was the Triassic Period. The dinosaurs made their first appearance. The New Red Sandstones, seen throughout much of north-west England, including the fringes of Cumbria, were laid down at this time.

The Jurassic Period followed, beginning 200 million years ago. By then the British Isles were covered in sub-tropical forests and shallow seas, rich in animal life, including ammonites and dinosaurs. Jurassic rocks can be found in a wide stretch running from the North Yorkshire coast down to the beaches of Dorset but all have disappeared from the Lakeland region.

And then for a while, the shallow seas gained ascendancy. This was the dawn of the Cretaceous Period, beginning about 145 million ago. Now the British Isles found themselves about 40 degrees north, roughly the same latitude of Spain today.

As the Cretaceous seas deepened and covered more and more of the British Isles, including the Lake District, the only sediments reaching the sea floor were those of calcareous, limey planktons and silica-rich sponges. Over millions of years, these slow accumulating lime-rich muds eventually formed the brilliant white rock we know now as chalk. Most of the chalk we see today is found in a swathe running south from North Yorkshire and then expanding to cover much of south-east England. Long since worn away, there are no examples of this distinctive white rock to be found in the Lake District. The Cretaceous Period ended 65 million years ago and with it the end of the dinosaurs.

Other things of great geological importance were also taking place during these late Cretaceous times. The fused tectonic plates of Laurentia and Eurasia, with the British Islands sandwich in the middle, began to split apart. The mantle's upward flowing convection currents deep below the plates began to diverge and spread, pulling the old Laurentian plate of North America off in a westerly direction. The rift that opened up was slightly further west than where the old Iapetus Ocean had been back in Cambrian and Ordovician times. The old suture line that had stitched Scotland and England together remained strong. Into the widening rift, out west beyond Ireland and the Hebrides, the seas began to pour. This was the birth of the Atlantic Ocean and it took place around 54 million years ago.

The rift where the two plates of Europe and North America were pulling apart was a place of volcanoes, basalt lavas, fresh ocean crust and new islands. Around 50 million years ago this volcanism was most active in Northern Ireland and along the north-western margins of Scotland, helping to form such places as the Giant's Causeway, Ardnamurchan, and the isles of Mull and Skye.

All this tectonic activity in the region of the North-east Atlantic also caused a slight tilting upwards of much of the western side of the British Isles, including the Lake District and all the younger sediments that had long overlain the old Skiddaw Slates and Borrowdale Volcanics. This uplift meant that rain and rivers could begin to erode the chalk and sandstones, shales and grits, coals and limestones, so that today we find little evidence of their once widespread presence over the ancient rocks of the central Lakes. They've nearly all been weathered away.

The rifting that started the separation of America from Europe is still active today. As we saw above, the Mid-Atlantic Ridge defines the line where the two plates are currently pulling apart. America's drift west continues, roughly at the rate of 5 centimetres a year, 5 metres a century, 50 kilometres every one million years.

The era following the Cretaceous – the current one in which we still find ourselves – has been named the Cenozoic, from the Greek meaning 'new life'. This was the age when mammals began their rise. It is within this period that we find rocks that used to be known as the Tertiary. They are aged between 65 and 2.5 million years and are mainly found in the south-east of England.

Meanwhile, far to the south, another tectonic plate had also been on the move. Some 40-odd million years ago the great African plate was beginning to nudge north. This heralded its slow, unstoppable push into southern Europe. The rocks and sediments caught up in its crash zone began to lift and buckle. The result was a new mountain chain – the Alps – which is still on the rise today.

Our part of the world was not immune from Africa's push north. Beyond the major crumple zone of the Alps, less dramatic movements rippled north. These far-ranging ruptures produced gentle folds and domes in rocks way beyond the northern edges of the Alps, including the rocks of the British Isles. The undulating landscape of the chalk Downs was one result. Another was the gentle doming of the younger sedimentary rocks that had been deposited on top of the old Ordovician metamorphic and volcanic rocks of the Lake District.

The rainwaters flowing off this gentle Cumbrian dome flowed down from the central heights creating a radial pattern of river drainage. Over the next tens of millions of years, the wind, rain and sun weathered away the overlying younger rocks but the radial drainage pattern remained as it was gently lowered onto each successive layer of increasingly older rocks below until eventually the ancient rocks of the Skiddaw Slates and the Borrowdale Volcanics once more found themselves back on the surface, where we see them today. Scientists call the inherited pattern of rivers and lakes being gently lowered onto the central fells 'superimposed drainage'.

The mountains of the mighty Caledonides 400 million years ago have long been worn away. Their remains have been covered and recovered by deposits of younger sediments. The old, tough rocks of the Ordovician Period offered more resistance to the processes of erosion than the younger, softer chalks and siltstones. They now stand ancient and proud above the surrounding lowlands. Even so, although the major rock groups of Skiddaw, Borrowdale and Windermere trend roughly north-east to south-west, the dome-like topography of the Lakes remains as one of the long-term legacies of Africa ploughing into Europe and causing ever-smaller waves and minor bumps to ripple across northern Europe.

And then, two and a half million years ago, it began to snow. Heavily. For a long time.

Chapter 12

ICE

I'd forgotten how narrow the path and sharp the drop is on either side of Striding Edge. It's been several years since I last took the track from Patterdale to climb the summit of Helvellyn. Maybe it's an age thing, but I'm feeling a little anxious as I peer down to the black waters of Red Tarn to my right and the even steeper fall to Nethermost Cove on my left. Thankfully the wind is light, the clouds are high, and I've forgotten the story of Charles Gough and his little dog, Foxie.

All around me are the explosive rocks of the Upper Borrowdale Volcanic Group. The sharp, precipitous divide of Striding Edge itself is an arête. This is a glacial feature, and although the rocks on which I am carefully edging my way along may be nearly 500 million years old, the carving of the arête is, geologically speaking, new and fresh.

Striding Edge was honed during the last Ice Age, a time when the Lake District, along with the rest of northern Europe, including most of the British Isles, was covered in a vast ice sheet, up to 2,300 feet or 700 metres thick in parts. The present drama of the Lake District is the result of tough, resilient rocks formed half-a-billion years ago being sculpted by ice, wind and rain, but particularly ice.

Every few hundred million years, planet Earth chills and suffers a major ice age. There have been at least five over the last 2 or 3 billion years. The most recent of these is known as the Quaternary Ice Age. It's the one that has shaped the landscape of the British Isles as we currently know it and, technically, is the one in which we still find ourselves today. It began about 2.5 million years ago and it defines the present major geological period.

What causes ice ages is still a matter of debate. Likely culprits include changes in the Earth's orbit and axis around the sun, the Earth's 22,000-year cyclical wobble, the movement and position of the continents caused by plate tectonics, how the ocean's currents switch and swirl between and around continents, and how much carbon dioxide and methane there is in the atmosphere. It's likely that there are complex interactions between all these elements. But when temperatures drop and the snows begin to fall, and when the summers get colder and not all the winter snows melt, glaciers form and grow, and ice sheets begin to spread. And just over two million years ago one of these chilly combinations began to take shape.

To complicate matters further, during any one major ice age, there can be a number of warm bursts. These *interglacial* warm phases can last tens of thousands of years, sandwiched between the long, very cold spells. Over the last 2.5 million years, the Quaternary ice sheets have therefore waxed and waned over the British Isles many times.

Today, we are in one of the relatively warm interglacial periods, but with the distinct possibility that another cold glacial spell will sweep the planet in the next 30-odd thousand years, although of course man-made global warming is the new joker in the Earth-history pack and who knows quite what will happen next.

In Britain and northern Europe, the biggest of the Quaternary ice advances happened around 450,000 years ago. It is known as the Anglian Ice Sheet. It stretched as far south as the current Thames and Severn valleys in a line running roughly between London and Bristol. If I was standing on Helvellyn all that time ago I might find myself on an outcrop of rock that is just managing to pierce the ice and snow. All around me, as far as the eye could see, would be glaciers, ice sheets and the frost-shattered peaks of the Cumbrian mountains.

If the Anglian glaciation was the biggest of the Quaternary ice advances, the most recent was the Devensian, which began around 100,000 years ago. This last ice advance began, like all ice advances, when global temperatures once again began to plummet. In northern Europe, the winter snows fell more heavily, especially over the mountains. The summers were no longer warm enough to melt the winter drifts. The snows compacted and slowly turned to ice, and ice – like water – flows downhill, but slowly, glacially slow.

Over the mountains of the Lake District, Wales, the Pennines, Scotland and Scandinavia the rivers of ice glided and ground their way down the pre-existing river valleys, out onto the plains, merging to form vast ice sheets. Under their own weight, the sheets spread out in all directions, covering much of the land, and then out over the dry Irish and North Sea basins. At their most extensive, these Devensian ice sheets formed a wilderness of white from Ireland to Norway. More modest than some of its Quaternary predecessors, nevertheless it still covered the northern half of the British Isles. Its last maximum was around 18,000 years ago and its icy reach just about touched the northern fringes of the Midlands plains.

To the south of the ice sheet, cold, wind-blasted tundra lands stretched from southern Ireland, across southern England, the lands that are now the southern North Sea, across to the continental plains of Europe. At its peak, there was so much water locked up in the huge ice caps that sea level was over 325 feet (100 metres) lower than it is today. There was no Irish or North Sea, only ice to the north and tundra to the south.

As the climate continued to cool, more and more snow fell over the mountains of the Lake District. Glaciers began their inexorable flow down the valleys. Above the rivers of ice, frozen mountain peaks shattered in the extreme frosts. The scree-littered summits of Scafell Pike and Bow Fell offer fine examples of the power of frost and ice to break up even the hardest of rocks. Much of the scree tumbled down the mountains, skirting the slopes. And some of it eventually fell onto and into the ice below.

Thus, the glaciers became armed with the splintered, fractured remains of the mountain summits. With their rocky cargo, they could now scour and scrape, chisel and gouge, smooth and polish, file and flow their way down the old river valleys and slopes, accentuating their width and depth. Along many of the valley bottoms today you can see massive outcrops of rock that bear evidence of the glacier's rasping flow. The rocks are relatively flat and ice-smoothed. But many are scratched by hundreds of fine lines all running in close parallel along the axis of the valley. These are known as 'striations', lines etched by the rocky remains entombed at the base of the slow-moving ice.

And on the glaciers flowed, joining forces with other frozen rivers, to form massive ice sheets until eventually they slipped and slid across the plains and river basins, carrying their booty of ground rock and shattered stone plundered from far and wide.

Let's just pause a moment and retrace the path of these glaciers as they flowed slowly down from their mountain heights. It was as these rivers of ice made their journey that much of the mountain scenery we see today was shaped. Prior to the ice and glaciers, the Lake District was a domed land weathered by rain and eroded by rivers. The hills and valley would have had a more rounded, softer feel to them. But the cold, ice and snow changed all that.

The heads of the valleys where the glaciers were born carve great scoops into the high mountain sides. There they formed deep hollows known as 'corries' or 'cwms'. Today, many of these mountain bowls are filled with water creating the high tarns that delight the fell walker. Stickle Tarn, Blea Water in the High Street fells, Grisedale Tarn, Angle Tarn. When the clouds are low and the light is grey, there is a sense of mystery as you come across a tarn resting quiet, timeless and still in the misty mountain air.

As several glaciers can form around a mountain's summit, a number of corries can be scooped and scraped around one peak. Where two deep-sided corries cut back and intersect each other, a sharp edge or rocky dividing line is created. This is known as an arête, and it is along the Striding Edge arête that I am precariously walking as I make my way towards the summit of Helvellyn. Further north, the very name of Sharp Edge on Blencathra tells you of its glacial origins.

Of the fifty or more corries in the Lake District, most face north-east. At the beginning of the Ice Age, sides of the mountains sheltered from the prevailing south-westerly winds allowed blown snows to collect and mass. Here the sun rarely shone. The snows turned to ice and the ice began to flow and the glaciers made their inexorable way down the mountains, into the valleys and out on to the plains of the Ice Age tundra. It might also be noted that it is this preponderance of corries scooped out on the north-eastern sides of the mountains that give many of the fells their typical asymmetric profile.

Many of the lower hills, such as Loughrigg Fell, Silver How and Lingmoor Fell have a rough, rocky, hummocky look to them. They are often puddled with small tarns and boggy pools. Geomorphologists describe this kind of terrain as 'knock and lochan', classically seen in the North West Highlands of Scotland. It results from ice sheets flowing over, tugging and plucking at weaknesses in the rock beneath leaving behind a fellscape that looks rummaged and roughed up.

Being of greater volume and more powerful than rivers, the glaciers widened and deepened the valleys giving them a characteristic

'U' shape in cross section, although in the case of the Lake District the valleys tend to adopt a more open, relaxed 'U', with less severe sides than say the ice-carved valleys of the Alps. Valley bottoms in the Lake District are typically flat; Borrowdale, Great Langdale and Buttermere are good examples. And because glaciers, unlike rivers, can gouge long and deep, and even scrape below sea level, when they melt they leave behind them depressions that are soon filled by rivers to form the ribbon lakes that fan out around the central dome. Windermere, for example, occupies the hollowed-out valley formed when the glaciers sliding down Little Langdale and Great Langdale coalesced near Ambleside, where they were joined by the ice flowing south from the Helvellyn range as well as the glaciers slipping west along the Troutbeck valley.

* * *

About 18,000 years ago the planet once again began to warm, slowly at first. The retreating ice sheets and glaciers dumped their freight of rock scree, boulder clay and tills forming 'moraines'. These can be seen as the many low, rounded, grassy mounds and hummocks that you see along some valley floors. Examples occur in many of the major valleys including Borrowdale and Dovedale below Hart Crag. A little gathering of small moraines can also be seen beneath the Langdale Pikes gently undulating by Mickleden Beck.

I have a dream-like memory of walking along the Cumbria Way to the head of Great Langdale. It was early February. The low cloud cast a soft white light over the valley. There was not a breath of air. The grasses on the moraines were drained yellow-green in colour. And in the quiet I walked among the gentle rises and falls of the little hillocks. They looked and felt sensuous. For an hour or more I wandered slowly and silently over the rolling, voluptuous slopes of these ice-born clays and glacial rocks on this enchanted morning.

It was as the ice sheets melted that the seas began to rise once more. Frozen and scraped by the ice, the lands of the Lake District first emerged from their cold embrace naked and bare, shorn of soil and vegetation to reveal what, by and large, we see today. As Jonathan Otley observed, although wind and rain, ice and snow are the tools with which nature fashions the landscape, it is the character of the rocks on which they work that has determined the present look of the Lake District.

The Skiddaw slates, mudstones and siltstones have eroded to give us a rounded, relatively uniform skyline and topography. These compacted sedimentary and metamorphosed rocks weather evenly to create high fells with a relatively soft and smooth profile.

The many layers of andesite lavas in the Lower Borrowdale Volcanic Group have weathered into step-like hills, known as trap topography (after the German, *'trap'*, meaning step). High Rigg just south of Keswick offers a nice example. Even the original flow lines of the old lava bands can sometimes be made out, for instance on Hay Stacks (also written as 'Haystacks'). More generally, the mountain scenery produced by the rocks of the Lower Borrowdale Volcanics are fells that are broad and plateau-like in their topography, with boggy summits and steep, craggy slopes falling away precipitously down to the valleys below.

The peaks of the Upper Borrowdale Volcanic Group are generally higher and more rugged and ragged than those of the Lower Borrowdale Volcanic Group. They occur in the central, eastern and southern fells forming the peaks of Helvellyn, Scafell Pike, Bowfell, Crinkle Crags, Coniston Old Man and High Street.

The last major rocks to be laid down were the sedimentaries of the Windermere Supergroup. These include shales and sandstones, limestones and grits. They are softer and more easily eroded than their volcanic forebears. The result is the more gentle, subdued landscape of the southern Lakes. No craggy heights here. Grassy fields and leafy woods slope down to lakeside shores. It was the landscape of choice for the rich industrialists of the nineteenth century in which to build their luxury mansions, faux castles, classical follies and rolling lawns.

Once the ice began to melt, the trees and plants made their return. Seven or eight thousand years ago birch, hazel, oak, elm, lime and alder reappeared in the lower valleys. The woodlands gradually spread along the valley floors. Oaks and pines soon were cloaking the slopes of the fells up to heights of around 2,000 feet or 600 metres. By about 7,000 years ago the returning forests had managed to cover most of the Lake District. Only the very highest ground remained open and stony, shrub-patched and grass covered.

And then close on the rooted heels of the returning trees and plants, Neolithic men, women and their children followed. From around 6,000 years ago, the natural landscape gave way to one that was increasingly man-made as trees were felled, fields farmed and sheep grazed.

Chapter 13

STONE AGE TO IRON AGE

As far back as 14 to 15,000 years ago, the retreat of the ice began to see the return of Stone Age hunter-gatherers to parts of the British Isles. This was a time when people could roam, trade and travel freely across the plains of Germany, northern France and southern England, which was still connected to continental Europe by a vast land bridge known as Doggerland, now drowned under the shallow North Sea.

It was as the ice sheets melted that sea levels rose. The waters crept back into the Irish Sea, and edged their way over the North Sea basin and along the English Channel. It was around 9,000 years ago that the rising seas finally cut off the British Isles from mainland Europe. And still the climate continued to warm, and as it warmed, the ice sheets and glaciers of the central Lakes melted away, allowing more and more people to migrate north and west.

However, it was not until about 7,500 years ago that these ancient Britons finally reached the coastal fringes and lower valleys of the Lake District. This was towards the end of what archaeologists call the Mesolithic Period, or Middle Stone Age. A few hardy souls seemed to have settled even earlier. Findings from Kirkhead Cave near Morecambe Bay suggest some limited occupation as far back as 10,000 years ago or more, but significant settlements didn't begin to establish themselves until the end of the Middle Stone Age. Some of the first people to arrive had made their way across the plains of the North Sea just before it became inundated by the rising seas.

They had migrated west from the Baltic, Denmark, the Netherlands, Belgium and northern France.

As we saw at the end of the last chapter, by this time the Lake District was becoming thickly forested. Along the more accessible, fertile coastal fringes and in the lower valleys, there were deer and wild pigs in the woods, geese and wild fowl on the water, and fish in the rivers and lakes. There was plenty to hunt. Throughout the summer and early autumn the trees and bushes were laden with fruit and berries. Along the coast and around the estuaries there was sea-food and shellfish. There was plenty to gather.

Significantly, by the end of the Mesolithic Period, around 6,000 years ago, we see the beginnings of wood clearance and the growth of small settlements. This being the Stone Age, the skills to cut, knap and fashion hard, brittle rocks such as flint and volcanic tuffs into axes and spear heads continued to improve, meaning that forests could be cut and cleared for land and burnt for fuel. Wood could also be chopped and then worked into timber, for tools, for build-ing, for fences, for dug-out canoes. This was a time, then, when our ancient forebears began to farm and develop agriculture alongside their hunting, gathering and fishing.

The beginnings of farming and the gradual decline of free-roam-ing hunter-gatherers also introduced the concept of land-ownership and with it the idea of 'my land' and 'not your land', land that had to be protected and if necessary fought for.

Archaeologists have decided that the Neolithic Period – the New Stone Age – began about 6,000 years ago and ended around 4,300 years ago. Migration continued, including people who sailed in canoes from Ireland to settle along many of the western margins of northern England, the Lake District and southern Scotland.

Although there was still hunting and gathering, it was the wide-spread introduction of crop cultivation and the increasing number of permanent small settlements that began to define the New Stone Age. Weapons and tools became more refined. Pots were made. Cloth was woven. The land was farmed for cereals. Animals were kept for food, milk and skins. Trade within and between countries became more widespread. Indeed, the movement and resettlement of people across Europe was surprisingly fluid, all helping to diversify populations and mix up gene pools more than was once imagined.

One part of the Lake District became particularly important for Stone Age Britons. Even if they didn't appreciate the wonders of geological time, they certainly recognised a good rock when they saw one. And they saw one way up high on the steep slopes of Pike o' Stickle, one of the peaks of the Langdales. From between 6,000 and 4,000 years ago, this location became the major centre for the seasonal production of stone axes. Once the axes were roughed out in shape, they would be sent down to coastal settlements for polishing and finishing.

Today the Great Langdale site is regarded as one of the most important prehistoric axe factories in Europe. Axe heads from this location have been found all over England and Northern Ireland. I've always thought it was rather patronising to regard the Stone Age and its people as primitive – 'back in the Stone Age'. They were people busy developing new skills and technologies, beginning to manage and exploit the local landscape, and bartering and trading on an international scale.

The Langdale axes were fashioned from fine-grained, green Borrowdale Volcanic tuffs, known as greenstone. The axes were certainly used for practical purposes, but the rather beautiful pale, grey-green colour made them much sought after for decorative and ceremonial purposes too. It was the axes aesthetic value as much as their practical use that saw them traded up and down the land.

On my last visit to the outcrop, the wind was blowing hard and the rain was blasting down the valley. Dressed in my waterproofs and heavy walking boots, I stood on the high scree slopes looking down towards Mickleden Beck, buffeted by the gale. I simply couldn't imagine what work and life must have been like for the men, women and maybe even children who chipped, hammered and scrimmaged for the prized rock 4,000-odd years ago on these very hills. And then I began to wonder, what on earth were they doing up here in the first place? It does suggest they had an intuitive grasp of stones, minerals and their geological character, but being Stone Age folk I suppose they knew a thing or two about rocks.

* * *

The trade in greenstone axes began to bring relative wealth to the area. Throughout the ages the rich and powerful have been wont to flaunt their success by building big. Pyramids, triumphal arches, steeples, towers, skyscrapers – the tallest buildings often tell us who were the most powerful people in that age. Ancient pharaohs and kings built their pyramids and palaces. Medieval bishops and popes raised churches and cathedrals, spires and steeples. And in our own age, bankers and financiers commission thrusting skyscrapers and glassy towers.

Well, Neolithic chiefs might not have been able to build quite so big and tall, but wealth and prestige allowed them to build big and round. Late Stone Age Cumbria has a surprisingly large number of stone circles and henges. There are two henges near the village of Eamont Bridge, just south of Penrith. They are only a few hundred metres apart – the larger Mayburgh Henge and smaller King Arthur's Round Table. The earth-covered cobble-stoned banks of Mayburgh Henge are nearly 20 feet (7 metres) high and 400 feet (120 metres) across. Archaeologists have estimated that up to

20,000 tons of pebbles and stones were used to build the core of the circular embankments. That takes time, money, prestige, power and commitment.

Perhaps the most distinctive and evocative stone circle is the one sitting atop Castlerigg, just south of Keswick. The setting is glorious. The grassy plateau lies in the centre of a vast, mountainous amphitheatre. As you stand in the middle of the stones and slowly pan round you see High Seat, Helvellyn, Blencathra, Skiddaw, and in the distance, Scafell Pike. There is a sense of the sublime. I'm here on another wild, windy day. The broiling clouds, low and grey, tumble and swirl. For a mad moment I imagine I'm conducting the heavens as they rage in nebulous frenzy around and above my head.

There are around forty standing stones at Castlerigg. The tallest is over seven feet, two metres, in height. Some of the stones weigh as much as 16 tons. They are made of the local Skiddaw Slates. At its widest the circle measures over 100 feet (30 metres) across. Its age has been put at around 5,000 years.

Although the transition in terms of people and settlements would have been relatively seamless, the end of the Neolithic Age about 4,500 years ago marked the beginning of the Bronze Age. Recent ancient DNA studies reported in the journal *Nature* suggest that around this time large-scale migrations of pastoral nomadic people from the steppes of Asia were moving westwards into Europe, some eventually reaching Britain.

Because of their skill at making bell-shaped beakers, archaeologists have called them the Beaker people. Over the next few hundred years the Beaker folk gradually established themselves as the majority population, interbreeding with and replacing up to 90 per cent of the British gene pool as the pre-existing Stone Age population began to fail. As the geneticist David Reich reminds us in his book *Who We Are and How We Got Here: Ancient DNA and the New Science of the Ancient*

Past, the idea of race is a fluid one. There is constant mixing and remixing of peoples over time and across place.

The Bronze Age was the first time in human history that people had learned to extract metals by heating rocks rich in metallic mineral content. But not only that, they learned how to harden the softer metals that they had won by adding other metals to the molten mix. With harder metals, tools could be made and weapons fashioned.

Peoples in the Near East were the first to discover that by mixing molten copper with around 12 per cent of tin you could produce an 'alloy'. This is bronze, and it marked the beginning of the Bronze Age. The skills to make bronze quickly spread east to India and China, and west into the Mediterranean and the rest of Europe. It took a while before the technology eventually arrived in Cumbria. Here, stone tools continued to be used for many hundreds of years into the Bronze Age. Although some metal furnaces have been found, for example in Ewanrigg near Maryport on the west coast, for a while most bronze tools were acquired through trade rather than local manufacture. Eventually however, the knowledge and skills to make bronze were developed by local craftsmen. And again, with better axes, now made of metal, yet more trees were chopped down and larger fields opened up. Farming practices not only expanded during the Bronze Age, but also continued to improve. This meant that settlements became more permanent.

However, even though technological and agricultural practices continued to advance, ceremonial and burial practices still followed the traditions of their Neolithic ancestors. Bronze Age cairns, barrows and standing stone circles have all been found in the Lake District. Buried with the dead, the bereaved also placed ornamental beads, jet, pottery, pins and buttons made out of bone, and even knives, daggers and jewellery.

A rather beautiful stone circle, measuring 90 feet (27 metres) in diameter can be found on the slopes of Black Combe at Swinside, down in the south-west of the county. The late Aubrey Burl, archaeologist and megalithic monument expert, called the Swinside Stone Circle 'the loveliest of all the circles' in north-western Europe. Who am I to disagree? It is rather special, sited in quiet seclusion in a small field, by a dry-stone wall, beneath Black Crags with the silhouette of Black Combe in the distance. This is how Charles Parish described Black Combe:

> Close by the Sea, lone sentinel,
> Black-Comb his forward station keeps;
> He breaks the sea's tumultuous swell,—
> And ponders o'er the level deeps.

Around 3,000 years ago, possibly in the Caucasus region between the Black and Caspian seas, people next discovered how to smelt iron from various iron-rich rocks. Iron was stronger and more versatile than bronze. It soon began to replace the copper alloy in the manufacture of tools, farm implements, weapons and cooking utensils. Again, the technology spread west and quickly established itself throughout Europe. It arrived in Britain around 2,800 years ago and marked the beginning of the Iron Age.

Iron Age Celtic Britain spanned almost a thousand years, not ending until the Romans arrived. During this time, farming practices continued to improve and intensify. Field systems were developed. Boundary dykes and ditches were dug. House building designs and techniques became more sophisticated. Round-houses, with their circular shape and conical thatched roofs, were sometimes built with stone bases but more commonly they used wooden posts with walls made of wattle and daub. Hill forts were raised.

In Cumbria, the various Celtic tribes, including the Carvetii in the north and the Setantii in the south, possibly merged and became part of the Brigantes, a tribe that occupied much of Northern England including Lancashire, Yorkshire and County Durham. The lack of written records means that historians are still debating the exact details of how these various tribes were linked politically and practically, but there is no doubt that at this time relationships between the Celtic tribes of northern England were both busy and active.

A cooling of the climate at the end of the Bronze Age and the beginning of the Iron Age about 2,700 years ago probably made the Lake District less hospitable and farming more difficult, at least for a while. But then once more temperatures slowly began to recover. This allowed farming to return to the inland valleys and lower hills.

With improved axes now made of iron, even more woodland and forest was felled. Cereal production increased. Animals could graze and nibble more widely and extensively, with the added advantage, at least as far as the Iron Age farmers were concerned, of keeping reforestation at bay. All in all, this was a time of relative growth and prosperity. It has been estimated that the Celtic population of Cumbria towards the end of the Iron Age was possibly as high as 20,000 or more, with most families living in small, scattered farmsteads.

And then the Romans arrived.

Chapter 14

ROMAN ROADS TO
VICTORIAN RAILWAYS

Although Julius Caesar had made a flying visit to Britain in 55 BC, the Romans didn't seriously set about conquering the country until AD 43 when the Emperor Claudius sent his armies north. Battle by battle, they slowly conquered most of south-east England. After the defeat of Boudica, queen of the Iceni tribe in East Anglia, the Romans continued to progress north and west. For several decades, Cumbria remained independent of Roman rule but by AD 79, the Brigantes were finally overcome by an army led by Julius Agricola.

The Romans, being Romans, quickly built roads and defensive forts. The roads allowed the occupying forces to communicate quickly over distances and speedily move men to wherever they were needed. I confess I've driven, rather than hiked or biked, to see the Roman Fort at Hardknott Pass. Standing among the stone ruins I'm trying to imagine what it must have been like for the men stationed at this far-flung garrison of the Roman Empire in the second century AD. It's an unlikely setting. Perched over 800 feet (250 metres) above the River Esk, it has commanding views down the valley. The Roman fort and harbour town of Glannoventa, now modern-day Ravenglass, lay ten miles west down the valley.

At first glance, the whole idea of building a substantial fort seemingly in the middle of nowhere seems hard to fathom. But of course historians have given us an explanation, and a fascinating one it is too. The Lake District was at the outermost edge of the Roman Empire and it was seen as something of a Celtic backwater. The Roman occupation was primarily military in nature. In order to keep the main north–south route to Carlisle open, it became important to suppress any hints of resistance from the Brigantine tribes who lived in the hilly and watery west. In contrast, the Celtic tribes in the south and east of the country experienced much more of the civil and cultural side of Roman life, and large towns, villas and temples were built. In these areas, Romans and Roman influences became much more integrated into everyday Celtic life.

In the less tamed, potentially troublesome Cumbrian edge of the empire, the need for a major east–west road soon became apparent to the occupying Roman forces. Roman road building engineers often took advantage of existing ancient routes, many originally pioneered by Neolithic and Bronze Age men and women. The local trade in axe heads and other products across the Lake District had already created routes that ran west to the sea as well as tracks to the east linking up with the Eden valley, and other major north–south roads.

By the beginning of the second century AD, construction began on building a road, known as the Tenth Iter, connecting Kendal, Ambleside and then over the hills to Ravenglass on the coast. The stretch between Ambleside and Ravenglass must have been challenging even for experienced Roman engineers. After weaving its way by the River Brathay, the road followed Little Langdale valley and then rose sharply up and over the Wrynose and Hardknott passes, reaching heights of over 1,200 feet (390 metres). It's on its descent into Eskdale that the road met the fort at Hardknott.

The fort was known as Mediobogdum by the Romans. It was built during the reign of Emperor Hadrian (AD 117–138), possibly by troops from Dalmatia, now modern-day Croatia. It is strategically well placed, surrounded by high crags and deep ghylls. At the site, there was a house for the commander, barracks for hundreds of men, granaries, a bath house, and, a little way up the hill, a parade ground.

At the Ambleside end of the road there was another Roman fort. Although the location of the Hardknott fort is more spectacular, Ambleside must have seemed a more attractive posting for the soldiers. Galava, as it was known, was built on the banks of the River Rothay just before it flows out into Windermere. The ground is low and flat. Loughrigg Fell rises to the west and Wansfell Pike to the east.

I often climb up to Todd Crag overlooking Ambleside. The view south is wonderful. Windermere stretches into the distance, rippled by lake cruisers, sparkled by the sun. Immediately below the fell are the remains of Galava, mapped out in stone. And like its counterpart at Hardknott, the garrison had a house for the commander, a courtyard, a couple of granaries, barracks and stables. There is also evidence of a small temple and an armoury. Pottery found on the site suggests the fort was occupied until around AD 383.

When the summers have been long, hot and dry, the parched grass etches out the Roman road that entered and left the fort on its way south to Kendal near where the next fort was sited.

There was another road that connected Galava to Penrith. Again, it probably followed tracks originally tramped out by the Ancient Britons as they sought routes to trade across the region. Soon after leaving the southern margins of Ambleside the road turns north, climbs up to Troutbeck and then along Hagg Gill. From here on for the next ten miles or more, the road becomes heroic. We now know it as High Street. Both the road and the plateau-like ridge take the same name. At its highest the Roman Road tops nearly 2,700 feet (over 800 metres). It marches on by High Raise and there, on your right as you head north, you see Haweswater a couple of thousand feet below. Of course, the Roman soldiers would have gazed down on a smaller lake than the reservoir we see today. And finally, and no doubt exhausted, you descend gradually down towards Penrith, the next Roman garrison town, twenty-five miles later.

Throughout most of Roman time, Cumbria continued to be a place of farming and scattered settlements, especially along the fertile coasts and the lower valleys. Small towns grew around some of the more congenial Roman forts at Penrith, Ravenglass and Watercrook just south of Kendal. But by and large the local Celtic people were left to get on with their lives, so long as they didn't cause trouble. Those closest to the forts would have provided the Roman garrisons with food, animal hides, pots and worked metals. Those further away might have had little to do with the occupiers.

In this part of the world, artistic and cultural Celtic traditions continued pretty much as before, experiencing only the lightest of influences from Rome and her ways. It must be remembered that many of the Roman soldiers were drawn from the Empire's provinces, including Gaul, Spain and Dalmatia. After twenty-five years' service a soldier would receive Roman citizenship. A few, no doubt, would have remained, settling in Cumbria, marrying local Celtic girls, having Romano-British children, fragments of whose DNA might still be found diluted in the genetic make-up of some current-day Lakelanders.

Although the Roman occupation of England and Wales continued for a couple more centuries, by AD 300 the decline of its over-stretched empire was well underway. North of Hadrian's Wall and west along the coasts, raids by the Picts and Scots became more frequent. Support for the Cumbrian-based Roman forces became less reliable before finally disappearing altogether. AD 410 marked the end of Rome's weakening hold over Britannia. The men and women of Cumbria once again were left to look after themselves.

* * *

After the fall of the Roman Empire the local Celtic people of western Britain called themselves 'Combrogi' or 'Cymri', meaning 'Fellow Countrymen', from which the old county name Cumberland, the land of the Cymri, ultimately derives. The Welsh word *Cymru* for Wales has a similar origin. Cymru and Cumberland, Celtic brothers and sisters.

Many place names still reflect these ancient Celtic links – Penzance, Penryn (Cornwall); Penmaenmawr, Pen-Y-Bont (Wales); Penrith, Penruddock, Pennington (Cumbria). The blen in Blencathra derives from the Celtic *blaen*, meaning point or top. Many of the names we still use for the region's rivers and streams have Celtic origins – Cocker, Derwent, Esk and Eden.

Between AD 410 and the Norman Conquest in 1066, the British Isles were invaded repeatedly, first by the Saxons from Northern Germany and Denmark and then later in the ninth century by the Vikings from Norway. The Celtic tribes of Cumbria were not immune from these invasions. Attacks came from both Celts north of the border and warriors from overseas. In the sixth century Rheged emerged, a Celtic kingdom covering modern-day Cumbria and Dumfriesshire and bits of Yorkshire. Rulers came and went. But by the beginning of the seventh century the power of Celtic Britain was in decline. The local Celtic populations were gradually scattered and battered by successive waves of new settlers.

From AD 600 onwards, the Anglo-Saxon kingdom of Northumbria spread west and eventually annexed the Celts of Rheged, although Celts who lived deep among the central mountains probably managed to have little contact with the invaders. The Cumbric language was gradually replaced by Anglo-Saxon. Nevertheless, as we've noted, a few of the more stubborn Celtic names did manage to persist. Most books on historic Cumbria mention that until fairly recently the numbers used by Cumbrian farmers to count their sheep harked back to Celtic times – *yan* (one), *tyan* (two), *tethera* (three)...

The last Celtic king of Cumbria was Dunmail. He died in battle as he fought the English Saxon King Edmund and the Scottish King Malcolm in AD 945. Legend has it that the site of the battle and his death was at Dunmail Raise, between Grasmere and Thirlmere. A pile of stones marks the spot where he died, or so it is said and so Wordsworth believed:

> And now have reached that pile of stones,
> Heaped over brave King Dunmail's bones;
> He who had once supreme command,
> Last king of rocky Cumberland;
> His bones and those of all his Power,
> Slain here in a disastrous hour!

Evidence of the Anglo-Saxon occupation of Cumbria also lingers in many of the county's place names. The Anglo-Saxons preferred arable farming to sheep rearing. Their ancestors had come from the flatlands of East Anglia, Denmark and the plains of northern Germany, so they tended to settle in the low, fertile edges of the Lakeland dome. Hill farming and sheep grazing by the lakes and in the mountains was probably left to the Celtic Britons. Any town or village whose name ends in '-ton' or '-tun' or '-ham' or which have '-ing' in their composition hint at Saxon origins. Addingham, Brigham, Workington, Stainton to name just a few. The suffix 'wic' suggests a place where things were made or sold. Keswick, for example, was a place that made cheese.

Anglo-Saxon domination of Cumbria lasted for over 200 years. But then throughout the eighth, ninth and particularly tenth centuries a new set of invaders attacked and occupied many of the coastal regions of Britain and Ireland – the Scandinavian Vikings, the Norsemen. The Norsemen who eventually settled in Ireland and probably intermarried with the local Irish Celts became known as the Norse-Irish. It was these men and women who sailed across the Irish Sea and began to explore and settle in Cumbria. Those who did make their home here were attracted to the higher dales and hills, those areas that didn't appeal to the Anglo-Saxons.

Up in the valleys and along the fells, the Norsemen with their Viking ancestry introduced new farming practices to the region. They knew how to rear cattle and sheep in these more rugged terrains. More land was cleared of forest and shrub. Studies of lake-deposited pollens from these times show a marked decrease in oak and a sharp increase in grasses, bracken and heather.

Ice-dumped boulders were removed from the valley floors to create more even grazing ground. The Norsemen built dry stone walls to divide fields and mark boundaries. They had advanced skills in ironwork, weaving and stone carving. Theirs was a more rugged culture, well-suited to their adopted home. And slowly, the Norsemen tamed and tidied the wilderness, helping to create the landscape that we know today.

The wide, bare, treeless horizons we see now are the result of centuries of wood clearance, cattle rearing and sheep grazing, which began in Neolithic times and were almost complete by the twelfth and thirteenth centuries. Landscape geographers Roy Millward and Adrian Robinson ruefully remind us that the Lakeland which Wordsworth celebrated, a world that he saw as 'unsullied by man' was, in truth, as much man-made and sheep-grazed as it was fashioned by the forces of nature.

Although the ninth and tenth century incursions by the Scandinavians undoubtedly had a significant impact on mountain life, the indigenous British Celts still remained one of the major ethnic groups to occupy the central lakes and higher hills. However, as the years passed, more and more integration between the different groups took place. By the early eleventh century the people of the Lake District were becoming more homogenised. Collectively, they could claim descent from Ancient Britons, the Anglo-Saxons and the Norse-Irish Vikings.

Modern-day DNA studies reveal an even more fascinating picture of the genetic origins of British people, with less mixing than you might think. For example, as you might expect, there is a higher percentage of Anglo-Saxon DNA in the people of the lowlands of eastern England. It ranges between 10 and 40 per cent suggesting a degree of intermarriage with the local Celtic population.

By contrast, separate, distinct and different genetic clusters are found all along the old western Celtic fringes of Britain, including a distinctive cluster found in the Cumbrian region. Sprinklings of Viking ancestry do occur throughout Britain as a whole, but amounts are surprisingly thin. So much for rape and pillage. However, for some reason Viking DNA levels are relatively elevated around the Penrith area compared to the rest of Cumbria. Make of that what you will.

And just to anticipate the Norman Conquest and any ideas that each foreign invasion involved a major dilution of ancient British stock, here is the conclusion from Professor Peter Donnelly and colleagues of the Wellcome Trust Centre for Human Genetics and their major study of the genetic history of the British Isles reported in 2015 (also see Leslie et al. in the bibliography):

> many ... major invasions of Britain have left very little genetic trace. We see little genetic evidence of the Roman conquest, nor of the Danish Viking control of large parts

of England from the 9th century ... nor of the Norman Conquest. These invasions have had a major impact on our history and culture, but not on our gene pool. The inference is clear. In each case there must have been control by a ruling elite, backed by a superior military power, but not large-scale settlement ...

Much archaeological evidence ... relates to the successful elites in society. In contrast, genetic evidence tells us about what has been happening to the masses.

So cultures and linguistic influences survive in the history books and the records of the rich and powerful. Even if the Vikings didn't mix that much with the local Britons, in the Lake District at least many Old Norse words have left their legacy.

'Beck' is from *bekr* for stream. The Norse for waterfall is *fors* from which we get 'force'. *Dalr* becomes 'dale'. The word *fjall* for hill evolves into 'fell'. Smaller hills and bluffs were known as *haugr* which we see today in the dozens of topographical features with the name 'how' or 'howe' (from which the surname derives – yeah!). Small lakes were called *tjorns*, and so we have 'tarns'. The suffix 'thwaite', meaning a small clearing or meadow, crops up in the names of many hamlets and villages: for example, Rosthwaite in Borrowdale, Braithwaite west of Keswick, and Crosthwaite in South Lakeland. As well as sheep and cattle, pigs were also kept. These were allowed to snuffle and root in the woodlands. The Norse for swine was *svina*, and for pig it was *griss*. Hence we still have piggy-place names such as Swindale, Swinside, Grisedale, Grizedale and Grasmere.

* * *

Although William I successfully invaded southern England after the Battle of Hastings in 1066, it took several more years before the Normans gained control of the whole of Cumbria. For centuries the tribes and kings of southern Scotland had fought over the lands of the Lake District. Indeed, for several decades prior to the conquest much of the region had been under the rule of Malcolm III of Scotland. However, towards the end of 1066, the southern Lakes fell to the Normans. The second Norman king, William 'Rufus' II then slowly began to extend his control northwards. In 1072 he took Carlisle, began to build a castle there in 1092, and by the end of the eleventh century all of Cumbria found itself under Norman rule.

Like their Roman predecessors, the Normans were wont to build castles both to defend and dominate their towns. They were also keen on building churches, abbeys and monasteries. Cumbria offers many examples of early monasticism: Carlisle Priory, Cartmel Priory and Shap Priory to name just a few.

However, in the first few centuries after the Norman invasion most of Cumbria's churches were built in the towns and villages on the edges of Lakeland's central dome. For those who lived among the lakes and higher hills, this meant a walk of ten or more miles to the nearest church. The other implication of this peripheral positioning was that when you died your body had to be carried some distance before it could be buried in the nearest church and its graveyard, and this gave rise to what became known as 'coffin roads'. The deceased were taken by packhorse or even sledge along well-trodden tracks. Until 1586 the Coniston dead were buried at Ulverston. In medieval times the nearest burial ground for those who died in and around Grasmere was Kendal, before ground was eventually consecrated in Grasmere itself. This meant that the final journey for those who passed away in Ambleside was particularly beautiful, the coffin route slowly winding its way by lakes, rivers and hills. Today the Ambleside to Grasmere stretch of this track remains one of the Lake District's most popular low-level walks. On days that are still, the views across Rydal Water offer a deep sense of rest and peace.

Throughout medieval times, more and more of the Lake District's land was carved up between the ruling feudal families and the great monastic houses, including Furness Abbey. These new landlords were intent on making the hills and dales productive. And so more trees were felled to provide charcoal for the iron smelters of Furness and space for sheep and their wool. Valley floors became better drained so more crops could be grown. As the peasants toiled, so their Norman rulers and priests got richer. 'Twas ever thus.

Fair to say though, the twelfth and thirteenth centuries saw a gradual increase in prosperity throughout the Lakes evidenced by the growth of small market towns. For example, Cockermouth gained the privilege of holding a market in 1227, and fifty years later in 1276 Keswick secured the same right. Then progress came to a sudden halt.

In spite of the Norman successes in the south of the country, Cumbria had long remained a battleground between the kings of England and Scotland. Carlisle was retaken by David I, King of Scots in 1135. A couple of decades later in 1157, King Malcolm IV of Scotland, under pressure from Henry II, returned Cumbria to English control and we see a more determined effort to introduce feudalism into the region. Crudely this meant the imposition of a Norman aristocracy to rule over a British peasantry.

English control also saw the creation, for the first time, of the counties of Cumberland and Westmorland. Moreover, for a long time, indeed until the new county of Cumbria appeared in 1974, there was a section of the southern Lakes that was part of Lancashire. In 1092 the land between the Duddon and Windermere was granted to the powerful Norman earl, Roger of Poitou by William II. As the name suggests, the Three Shires Inn in Little Langdale, with its beautiful view across to Wetherlam and the Coniston Fells, lies roughly at the point where Cumberland, Westmorland and Lancashire met before the boundary reorganisation.

By the fourteenth century, conflicts between England and Scotland became even more frequent and intense. Cumbria in general, and Carlisle in particular, often found themselves in the firing line. For example, after the Battle of Bannockburn in 1314, an enlivened Robert the Bruce pushed his luck and unsuccessfully tried to take the town of Carlisle. One of Carlisle Castle's claim to fame is that it has endured more sieges, including the one attempted by Robert the Bruce, than any other place in the British Isles. It is a pretty formidable structure, even today. It is built of rust-red and grey sandstones, and for a few weeks in 1567 the castle's tower was the home of Mary Queen of Scots, held prisoner by Queen Elizabeth I. Even so, in spite of Carlisle's resistance, the marauding Scots of the fourteenth century achieved many destructive and plundering successes especially around the fringes of the Lakes. These troubled times resulted in lost growth and economic setbacks.

In later years, some of the most ferocious raids were made by the infamous Border reivers. 'Reive' is an old English word for 'rob' and that is what the reiver families did, on whichever side of the Scottish-English border they lived. War between the two nations continued to make life along this boundary difficult. Raids across the border against ostensible enemy lands were frequent. Cattle and sheep were rustled. Houses and farms were robbed. The reivers attacked with speed. Their horsemanship became legendary.

It was not until 1603 when the crowns of England and Scotland were united in the person of James I that Cumbria was finally free of the warring fancies of English and Scottish monarchs. Gradually, the notorious raids by the Reiver families stopped. Nevertheless, over subsequent years their lives and exploits have been romanticised by many, including Sir Walter Scott. Here is the first stanza of a piece by a poet on the exploits of Jock o' Side published in *The Border Magazine*.

> O who will up an' ride with me:
> Come a' ye reivers bold!
> Then let us off to Cumberland
> To herry byre an' fold.
> We winna leave a horn or hoof
> On a' the English side,
> Then come, my bonny reivers,
> Come, let us mount an' ride.

* * *

More settled times allowed the Lake District to develop its strengths. Throughout the seventeenth and eighteenth centuries, Cumbria's farms, mines and industries continued to grow and expand. And, at last, the beauty of the landscape began to be recognised. The area's biggest asset – its lakes and mountains – was ready to be appreciated by a burgeoning tourist industry. But the idea that the rugged, rocky hills, the lowering clouds and the rushing waters were in any way 'romantic' took a while to take hold. For much of its pre-Georgian history, the Lake District was seen as a wild, uncivilised place, best avoided by the genteel classes. In his visit to the area in around 1720, the pioneering novelist Daniel Defoe – he of *Robinson Crusoe* fame – described the Lake District as 'being the wildest, most barren and frightful of any ... in England.'

However, slowly, what was once seen as dangerous and uncouth, began to be seen as wild and romantic. For some while the upper classes had been enjoying their grand tours of Europe. They had seen the majesty of the Alps. They had marvelled at cascading waterfalls. They had boated on glassy lakes. They had enjoyed adventures. And year by year, rather than avoid and skirt round the Lakes, the travelling classes began to wander into the valleys, ride by the lakes, and gaze at the mountains.

Encouragement to visit and explore was to be found in the words of poets and the paintings of artists. Fear turned to favour. Here, in 1767, quoted by Ian Thompson in his book on the history of the Lakes, is the reassuring Dr John Dalton of Wigton, capturing the change of mood from dread to delight:

> Horrors like these at first alarm
> But soon with savage grandeur charm
> And raise to noblest thoughts the mind.

It became progressively easier to visit the Lakes. Roads and transport links continued to improve. By the early nineteenth century, engineers were developing steam engines that ran on rails and could pull trucks and wagons.

Probably the most famous steam locomotive, *Rocket*, was built in 1829 in Newcastle by Robert Stephenson. Although by no means the first steam engine to run on rails, *Rocket*'s innovative design, power, economy and speed set the template for all other steam locomotives to follow. For several years, the engine ran between Liverpool and Manchester pulling passenger trains. Then between 1837 and 1841 *Rocket*'s life changed. Her work became rough and less glamorous. She was bought by James Thompson who had leased the colliery, limeworks and waggon ways from the Earl of Carlisle. The locomotive's job was to haul mineral-laden wagons along the lines of the Brampton Railway north-east of Carlisle. But the aging *Rocket* was no longer strong enough for such heavy work and she was eventually retired in 1841.

The power and efficiency of steam engines was improving all the time. By the 1840s, a railway building frenzy was well underway. Lines were laid down all over the country, owned, built and run by dozens of small, separate, speculative companies.

Although the Lancaster and Carlisle Railway did not originally pass through Kendal, there was a station built at Oxenholme a mile or so to the east. Pressure mounted to build a branch line that would pass through Kendal and on to Windermere. There was opposition, not least from William Wordsworth. He felt the railway would blight the beauty of his Lake District. And naturally he wrote a poem to that effect with lines that asked 'Is then no nook of English ground secure/From rash assault?' The sonnet ended:

> Speak, passing winds; ye torrents, with your strong
> And constant voice, protest against this wrong.

All of which is ironic given that it was Wordsworth's own romantic celebrations of the dales, lakes and hills that had made people want to see what he saw, and enjoy what he experienced.

His protestations, at least as far as building a branch line to Windermere were concerned, were to no avail. The line reached Windermere and its station was opened on 20 April 1847. It sits a couple of hundred feet above the lake, nearly a mile away. The original plan was to take the line on to Ambleside, hence the heightened location, but the extension never happened. What did happen was that the small hamlet known as Birthwaite at which the line actually terminated began to grow. Towards the end of the nineteenth century, Birthwaite decided to rebadge itself as Windermere, the town we know today.

A line to Coniston was built in 1859, and another across from Penrith to Keswick in 1864. By the beginning of the twentieth century, a necklace of railway tracks embraced the Lake District linking the coastal towns in the west with the north–south main lines connecting England and Scotland. From the roads the Romans built to the railway boom of Victorian Britain, the Lake District had gradually become more open, accessible and a place worth visiting.

Chapter 15

WHERE TO GO
AND WHAT TO SEE

For many early travellers the Lake District's scenery meant little. It hardly gets a mention in their journals. Travellers rarely stayed long in such a wild place; they merely passed through. Celia Fiennes, for example, wrote about her 'Great Journey to Newcastle and to Cornwall', in which she fleetingly passed through the Lakes in 1698.

However, by the mid-eighteenth century, people's sensibilities began to change. There was a gradual recognition that rugged landscapes could be romantic landscapes; rushing rivers, tumbling waterfalls and misty lakes could be beautiful. A letter, originally written to a friend by the Reverend Dr John Brown of Penrith, was published a year after his death under the title *A Description of the Lake at Keswick* in 1767. Although he was wont to exaggerate the scenery – 'horrible grandeur' and 'rude and terrible magnificence' – his was an early voice in what was to become known as the Romantic movement.

The poet and Cambridge professor, Thomas Gray, is often credited as being the first genuine Lake District tourist. In 1769 he travelled from Penrith, across to Keswick, along Borrowdale, and then south to Grasmere and Ambleside. His original plan was to stay at the Salutation Inn at Ambleside but he found it to be 'dark and damp as a cellar' so he carried on to Kendal. His ten-day trip led to some of the first fine writing about the Lakes. Here he is, in his *Journal of the Lakes*, describing Grasmere village and its nearby lake:

©HELEN HOTSON, SHUTTERSTOCK

One of Lakeland's most famous viewpoints: Ashness Bridge,
above Derwentwater, on the single-track road to Watendlath.

Blea Water, in the High Street fells: a corrie formed by glaciation.

Striding Edge, Helvellyn, a sharp ridge formed at the intersection or 'spine' of two corries.

Castlerigg Stone Circle, near Keswick.

Langdale, another glaciated valley and one of Europe's
foremost sites for Stone Age axe-production.

The Roman fort, Mediobogdum, at Hard Knott Pass.

Grasmere and Rydal Water were frequented by the Lake Poets.

William Wordsworth (by B.R. Haydon); Samuel Taylor Coleridge.

John Ruskin; Harriet Martineau.

Ullswater from above Patterdale, by John Parker, 1825.

A view over Coniston Water, by J.M.W. Turner, 1797.

Whilst many artists have painted glorious landscapes of the
Lake District, the illustrations by Beatrix Potter have attracted
tourists from around the world. Benjamin Bunny; Squirrel Nutkin
(top). Peter Rabbit; Flopsy, Mopsy and Cottontail (below).

Ambleside on Windermere is one of England's most-visited spots.

Sheep, it seems, are *everywhere* in the Lake District.

The bosom of the mountains spreading here into a broad bason [sic], discovers in the midst Grasmere-water; its margin is hollowed into small bays and bold eminences; some of rock, some of turf, that half conceal and vary the figure of the little lake they command: from the shore a low promontory pushes itself far into the water, and on it stands a white village with a parish church rising in the midst of it; hanging inclosures, corn-fields and meadows, green as emerald ... Not a single red tile, no gentleman's flaring house, or garden wall, break in upon the repose of this little unsuspected paradise; but all is peace, rusticity and happy poverty, in its neatest and most becoming attire.

Well of course, Grasmere is still a little paradise, but I'm not sure that on a busy summer's day all is still peace, and certainly not happy poverty. But Gray's appreciation awakened a new way of looking at the lakes and fells that has remained alive ever since. In his writings we begin to hear more of the early sounds of Romanticism in which nature and our responses to it were to become key themes. However, Professor Gray was not a brave man and the very thought of leaving the valleys and actually climbing a craggy mountain never entered his head. What he saw as he looked high into the fells 'was the turbulent chaos of mountain behind mountain, rolled in confusion.' Until the arrival of the Lakeland poets a few decades later, fell walking was mainly left to sheep and shepherds.

Equally influential was *A Guide to the Lakes in Cumberland, Westmorland and Lancashire* written in 1778 by Thomas West, another priest. He was born in Scotland, and in his younger days he travelled a great deal around Europe, before finally settling in Cumbria. His guide begins with these stirring words:

Since persons of genius, taste, and observation began to make the tour of their own country, and to give such pleasing accounts of the natural history, and improving state of the northern parts of the British Empire, the spirit of visiting them has diffused itself among the curious of all ranks. Particularly, the taste for one branch of a noble art ... in which the genius of Britain rivals that of ancient Greece and modern Rome, induces many to visit the lakes of Cumberland, Westmorland, and Lancashire; there to contemplate, in Alpine scenery, finished in nature's highest tints, the pastoral and rural landscape, exhibited in all their styles, the soft, the rude, the romantic, and the sublime; and of which perhaps like instances can nowhere be found assembled in so small a tract of country.

Who could resist the Lakes after this seductive invitation. He clinches the pitch by mentioning 'another inducement. ... The goodness of the roads, which are much improved since Mr Gray made his tour in 1765.' The guide also set the pattern for many later guides in the way that it was written and organised. The Lakes were discussed one by one. The landscape was described and various viewing 'stations' were recommended. West was also an early advocate of the idea of the 'picturesque'. Take, for example, his guide notes to Windermere:

Windermere-water, like that of Coniston, is viewed to the greatest advantage by facing the mountains, which rise in grandeur on the eye, and swell upon the imagination as they are approached.

So true. The guide was a major success. West's pioneering celebrations of the romantic; his descriptions of the sublime; and his advice on where to go, what to see and *how* to see it, set the fashion for 'scenic tourism'. The tourist industry had begun. It has remained one of the main money-spinners for the region and its economy ever since.

The Cumberland born cleric, artist and sometime headmaster of Cheam, William Gilpin, undertook a five day visit to the Lakes in 1772. He later described his impressions in a 1786 report catchily titled *Observations, relative chiefly to Picturesque Beauty, Made in the Year 1772, on several Parts of England; particularly the Mountains, and Lakes of Cumberland, and Westmoreland*. Certainly wordy, but the descriptions caught the imagination and once again introduced the idea of the 'picturesque'. Nature had to be viewed in terms of what was thought to be beautiful and picture-like. Not any old view would do. The sensitive traveller should choose those spots where the landscape composed itself most like a picture with beauty and drama.

Like Gray and West, Gilpin was not keen on exploring the actual mountains themselves. It was certainly not expected that genteel visitors should venture far from the safety of the 'viewing stations'. Although there were undoubted thrills in contemplating the high fells, there was still a lingering sense of danger and dread should one actually wander too far into the wild. But as we have seen, from Neolithic axe miners, to Roman road builders, to Medieval sheep farmers, the mountains were not only familiar to some people – they were also places of work.

In 1792 Joseph Budworth wrote an account of his 240-mile walk through the Lake District. It took him two weeks. He described himself as 'a rambler', on foot if not in word. He rambled up Skiddaw, Helvellyn, Helm Crag and Coniston Old Man. Realising that the touring classes would no longer fancy travelling through Europe because of the growing unrest in France, he turned his exploratory interests to Britain. He too was keen to take advantage of the growing fashion for all things 'picturesque'. His notes mention that he travelled in July and August. Luckily for him he enjoyed 'one fortnight of constant fine weather'. And he thought everyone and everything he saw was lovely including the locals whom he described as 'perfectly quaint', living their happy lives in a pastoral 'Arcadia'. He even managed to see a local production of *The Merchant of Venice* performed somewhere in Keswick in an 'unroofed house'. 'Some of the actors,' he writes, 'performed very well, and some very middling.' Budworth's records of actually climbing the peaks were among the first to introduce the idea of walking the fells for thrills and pleasure.

* * *

Ann Radcliffe was one of the most famous authors of the eighteenth century, her gothic novels were extraordinarily popular. Dostoyevsky wrote of the 'ecstasy and horror' he experienced as a child when he first read Radcliffe. She wrote of maidens in distress, dark and dangerous forests, and forbidding mists and mountains. The titles of her books conjure the terror and romance of the gothic: *The Mysteries of Udolpho*, *The Castles of Athlin and Dunbayne*, *The Romance of the Forest*.

She was also a great traveller and wrote about her 'tours' in a series of 'observations'. In 1794 Ann Radcliffe and her husband set off on a tour of the Alps. But these were troubled times in Europe. Sensing danger, they returned home and decided to explore, in relative safety, the Lake District instead. She wrote about her travels in an account entitled *Observations during a Tour to the Lakes of Lancashire, Westmoreland, and Cumberland*. However, even in her travel writing, the romance of the gothic was never very far from her manner and style.

They visited Brougham Castle where 'Dungeons, secret passages and heavy iron rings remain to hint of unhappy wretches'. They rode through the Vale of Keswick and climbed up to the stone circle at Castlerigg, where she imagined druids making savage sacrifices at the midnight hour. They tackled Skiddaw, a relatively tame walk up from Keswick, but in Radcliffe's eyes, it was a place of dark foreboding, even darker forces, and thrilling prospects. She wrote of 'tremendous chasms' and roaring torrents foaming down between the dark rocks. The view from the top was both commanding and 'dreadful' with Borrowdale seen in the distance, a place which she felt would offer a 'scene of tremendous ruin' and rocky danger. She recoiled from the view 'with involuntary horror.' Borrowdale, she felt, was a place where:

> Dark caverns yawn at its entrance, terrific as the wildness of a maniac, and disclose a narrow strait running up between mountains of granite that are shook into almost every possible form of horror, and resemble accumulations of an earthquake splintered, shivered, piled, amassed.

We'll forgive her geological ignorance, smile at the over-the-top gothic descriptions, and perhaps concede that she arrived in Borrowdale on a particularly wild and stormy day. But as Penny Bradshaw points out, in spite of some of the drama and hyperbole, what Ann Radcliffe did was introduce the idea that landscapes could induce powerful feelings in the beholder. Picturesque descriptions were all well and good, but there was emotion and romance to be felt and found on the fells, by the becks, and along the lakes. The early eighteenth century view that the passions should he constrained and held back to ensure a measured life was giving way to the idea that strong feelings could reveal deeper layers of our human experience. In this Ann Radcliffe anticipates the feelings and philosophy of the Lakeland poets who would follow a decade or so later.

This brings us back to Coleridge and Wordsworth, in particular Coleridge's description of his perilous descent of Scafell Pike via the ridge now known as Broad Stand that runs south-west to Scafell. The year was 1802. He was on a nine-day walking tour in which he would quite happily sleep out on the mountains each night. On the top of Scafell Pike, he noticed storm clouds heading his way. He decided to get down as quickly as possible. However, not knowing his way, he took what he thought was the most direct route which also proved to be the most hazardous. There were crags and vertical drops, narrow ledges and steep gullies. At times he said the sheer horror of his situation 'put my whole Limbs in a Tremble'. Coleridge found his feelings lurching between fear and mad exhilaration. But his romantic spirit never left him. The next day, clearly still excited, he wrote of his experiences in a letter to Sara Hutchinson:

> the sight of the Crags above me on each side, and the impetuous clouds just over them, posting so luridly and so rapidly northward, overawed me. I lay in a state of almost prophetic Trance and Delight ...

For those of us who enjoy scaling the rocky tops but whose sense of the vertical and our own mortality are all too strong, these feelings of fear and ecstasy, trance and delight are wonderfully familiar.

* * *

In spite of his anxieties about too many tourists and newcomers spoiling Lakeland, Wordsworth nevertheless found himself writing a guide for visitors. The original idea for a book about the Lake

District actually came from the Reverend Joseph Wilkinson. He married Mary Wood in 1788 and for a while the couple lived with the Brownriggs at Ormathwaite Hall near Keswick, before moving to Norfolk in 1804. He was an amateur artist and over the years had produced forty-eight engravings of the Lake District.

He thought it would be nice to have them printed and published, but he wanted some text to accompany the pictures. The vicar first approached Coleridge. The poet declined the invitation and suggested that the reverend artist ask Wordsworth, who needed the money. Wordsworth agreed. The text was not quite what Wilkinson was expecting. Wordsworth did not want to encourage a 'picturesque' approach to the lakes. 'My object,' he wrote, 'is to reconcile a Briton to the scenery of his own country'. He wanted people to appreciate the fells, rivers and lakes in all their subtlety and natural beauty. Nature, he felt, cannot be improved. This original guide appeared as *Select Views in Cumberland, Westmorland and Lancashire,* published in 1810, and although Wordsworth wrote the introduction to the vicar's engravings his name does not appear on, or in, the book.

However, having got a taste for such writing, Wordsworth decided to bring out a guide under his own name. The most successful edition – the fifth – of Wordsworth's *A Guide Through the District of the Lakes* was published in 1835. Its sales were steady but never spectacular, although they outsold his poetry. Wordsworth grew increasingly fond of 'my little Book on the Lakes'. To read it today is still a delight. At times Wordsworth can be rather conservative and didactic, telling the reader what to see and think, but his descriptions and enthusiasms feel timeless.

'It is hoped,' he writes, 'that this Essay may become generally serviceable, by leading to habits of more exact and considerate observation than, as far as the writer knows, have hitherto been applied to

local scenery.' As well as talk about what should be seen and under-
stood, Wordsworth was also keen to explain what it meant to live in
the area. His approach, says Jonathan Bate, 'was holistic: he moved
from nature to the natives, exploring the relationship between land
and inhabitant.' And then the poet sings of the beauty of the Lakes:

> I do not indeed know any tract of country in which,
> within so narrow a compass, may be found an equal vari-
> ety in the influences of light and shadow upon the sublime
> or beautiful features of landscape; and it is owing to the
> combined circumstances to which the reader's attention
> has been directed.

The guide is divided into a number of sections. It begins with
directions and how to get to places such as Windermere, Ambleside,
Ullswater and the Vale of Keswick. He then offers lovely descriptions 'of the Scenery of the Lakes' followed by 'View of the Country
Formed by Nature'. Having discussed nature's forms and beauty, he
then talks about 'Aspect of the Country as Affected by its Inhabitants'.
In this section he deals with the history of the area, its bridges, cottages, abbeys, churches, parks and mansions.

Even in the guide, Wordsworth's romantic roots kept pulling him
back to the idea of an ideal community based on notions of equality and cooperation. His ideas of a pastoral republic, an egalitarian
utopia, first explored with Southey and Coleridge, could be found
forty years later as he reminisces about the beauty of the traditional
ways of life:

> Towards the head of these Dales was found a perfect
> Republic of Shepherds and Agriculturalists, among whom
> the plough of each man was confined to the maintenance

of his own family, or to the occasional accommodation of his neighbour. Two or three cows furnished each family with milk and cheese. The chapel was the only edifice that presided over these dwellings, the supreme head of this pure Commonwealth; the members of which existed ... like an ideal society or an organized community whose constitution has been imposed and regulated by the mountains which protected it.

The most fun section of the guide, at least for the modern reader, he titles 'Change, and Rules of Taste for Preventing their Bad Effects'. Anticipating the Lake District National Park Authority a hundred years later, Wordsworth definitely had strong views about what should and shouldn't be built, planned and planted in Lakeland. And he definitely had a thing about larch trees.

The larch was first introduced into Britain from central Europe in the early years of the seventeenth century, partly for its timber. But when larch trees began their cultivated march across the fell-sides, obliterating native woodland, then, as Wordsworth said, 'mischief' was afoot. The introduction of plantations of fir and larch, he wrote, often causes 'great injury to the appearance of the country.' Wordsworth also had strong views about new buildings. These are his feelings and this is his advice:

in truth, no one can now travel through the more frequented tracts, without being offended, at almost every turn, by an introduction of discordant objects, disturbing that peaceful harmony of form and colour, which had been through a long lapse of ages most happily preserved.

No man is to be condemned for a desire to decorate his residence and possessions; feeling a disposition to applaud such an endeavour, I would show how the end may be best attained. The rule is simple; with respect to grounds – work, where you can, in the spirit of nature, with an invisible hand of art ...

Houses or mansions suited to a mountainous region, should be 'not obvious, not obtrusive, but retired;' ... Sir Joshua Reynolds used to say, 'If you would fix upon the best colour for your house, turn up a stone, or pluck up a handful of grass by the roots, and see what is the colour of the soil where the house is to stand, and let that be your choice.' ... The principle is, that the house must harmonise with the surrounding landscape ...

Wordsworth had a particular problem with houses painted white, at least until the white had faded and weathered. 'The objections to white, as a colour,' he believed, 'in large spots or masses in landscape, especially in a mountainous country, are insurmountable. ... Upon the whole, the safest colour, for general use, is something between a cream and a dust colour, commonly called stone colour.' Cottages should look as if they had grown naturally 'out of their native rock'. So there we have it. Avoid white and look to nature's palette of the subtle and subdued if you want to be architecturally sound and aesthetically inspired. I like that.

I have been a little mean in teasing out the poet's sterner and more decided views, sound as many of them undoubtedly are. Wordsworth's strength of character, backed by his evocative poems and prose, asserts itself on every page. The guide's advice on what to see and where to find it work as well today as it did nearly 200 years ago.

Wordsworth was also alert to changing tastes. There was a growing appetite for facts as well as fancy, science as well as scenery. Along with his poems he invited distinguished scientists to add essays, or 'letters' at the end of his guide. Professor Adam Sedgwick, for example, wrote about the geology of the region, while John Gough of Kendal, John Dalton's boyhood mentor, provided a section 'promoting' the botany of the Lakes.

* * *

For a few years, prolific writer and social reformer Harriet Martineau was a near neighbour of William, Mary and Dorothy Wordsworth. She was not a Cumbrian native, but for the last thirty years of her life she lived in Ambleside. Admiring her skills and reputation, Windermere bookseller John Garnett encouraged her to write a guide to the Lakes. This she did, and it was eventually published in 1855 as *A Complete Guide to the English Lakes*. Acknowledging her interest in the sciences in general and the latest ideas about the age of the Earth in particular, she even includes a lovely, soft-coloured geological map at the end of her book.

Unlike Wordsworth, and true to her socialist leanings, belief in progress and economic know-how, Martineau welcomed the railway. She thought its arrival would help stimulate the local economy as well as local minds, both of which she felt were in danger of flagging. Eight years after the arrival of the railways, she notes in her guide that since the arrival of Windermere railway station, there is now a Windermere post office, a hotel and a well-populated 'thriving village' whose:

> residents may find … that, their minds will have become more stirred and enlarged by intercourse with strangers who have, from circumstance, more vivacity of faculty and a wider knowledge.

The contents of Martineau's guide followed the established pattern with recommendations of where to go, what to see and what to do. She concludes with sections on 'Flowering Plants, Ferns, and Mosses' and for those who like to know these things, a 'Directory: The postal address of the Aristocracy, Gentry, and Tradespeople of the District'. There then followed a few pages of adverts for hotels and where to stay. Why not try Slater's Temperance Hotel, Ambleside where:

> Mrs. Isabella Slater
> Respectfully invites the attention of her Friends, Lake Visitors, and Tourists generally, to her Coffee and Tea establishment. ... Whilst strict economy is practised, no effort will be spared to promote the comfort and accommodation of those who may favour her with their patronage.

And depending on your pocket, for those who fancy the Furness Abbey Hotel, you can either enjoy a First Class Breakfast, with meat, for 1s 9d, or a Second Class Breakfast, with meat, for 1s 6d. I can't imagine what the difference would have been.

After taking one or more of her recommended tours, Martineau then advises the visitor 'to spend a day on the Mountains'. But which one, she wonders? Like many before and after her, she warns of the dangers of the higher fells. A map, she says, is essential. Have a pocket compass 'in case of sudden fog'. And as far as the more 'formidable' mountains such as 'Scawfell' (sic) and Helvellyn are concerned, 'always take a guide' – not a pocket-book guide but a local expert who knew his way around the hills.

In her chapter on the ascent of 'Scawfell' she talks about:

the fool-hardy ... who attempt the ascent without a guide. These last usually pay the penalty of their rashness in hours of uneasy wandering and excessive fatigue. When they think they see their way clearly enough, they are pretty sure to find themselves brought up on the verge of a chasm. ... If darkness comes on, there is nothing to be done but wait for daylight where they are.

Having warned of the dangers of climbing the highest peaks, she strongly suggests that the first-time visitor who wishes to ascend a mountain try something a little tamer. After considering and then dismissing Black Combe, the Old Man of Coniston, and the Langdale Pikes, she finally settles on Fairfield. 'The excursion is safe,' she says, 'not over-fatiguing, practicable for a summer day, and presenting scenery as characteristic as can be found. Let it be Fairfield.' And so there the reader has it. The sun is shining, the day set fair, there is no need for a guide. Then, indeed, let it be Fairfield.

* * *

The publisher John Murray's *Handbook: The Lakes, Westmorland and Cumberland, and the Lakes*, was first published in 1866. It went through seven editions and became a must for any visitor to the Lake District who wanted to 'contemplate the sublime or become rapturous over the picturesque'.

One of the most famous and successful of all the nineteenth century guides was M. J. B. Baddeley's *Thorough Guide to the English Lake District*. It was first published in 1880 and it went through many editions. He was against erecting signposts that showed the way to tracks and paths on the grounds that they would disfigure the landscape. Although Joseph Budworth a century earlier had talked of the thrills of rambling over the higher fells, Baddeley was one of the first systematically to describe routes both high and low. He was not afraid to recommend climbing the highest peaks. Every summit's rewards and dangers were discussed. In his willingness to consider high fells as well as low dales, he anticipated the twentieth century visitor's appetite for adventure as well as beauty and the picturesque.

Chapter 16

LOVE LETTERS TO
THE LAKE DISTRICT

Although I think Alfred Wainwright would sympathise with Baddeley's adventurous approach to the hills, I'm not sure what he would have made of Harriet Martineau's more cautious advice to take a guide when tackling the higher peaks. Wainwright was certainly mindful of safety. But he didn't see fell walking as a 'dangerous sport'. 'It is not a sport at all,' he says in his 2003 book *Memoirs of a Fellwanderer*. 'Those who utter grave warnings about it annoy me; they are doing a disservice.' Only the careless get into trouble. 'Fellwalking accidents happen only to those who walk clumsily. The only advice you need ... is to watch where you are putting your feet. Do this and you will not have an accident.' And certainly don't walk downhill on scree-strewn tracks and gawp at the view. If you want to admire the scenery, stop. You can't descend and gaze into the distance at the same time. 'For the third time,' he says, 'watch where you are putting your feet!'

The fells, he said, are not for fools but fools are all too often for the fells. They leap but don't look; they wander like lost souls in the mist; they break legs. 'As for common sense,' declaims Wainwright, 'well, some people haven't the sense they were born with. There is no hope for such folk and they should not go on the hills at all.' Harriet Martineau would agree.

Like Wordsworth and Martineau, Wainwright was a man of strong and definite views. His beautiful pocket-sized Pictorial Guides to the Lakeland Fells are known to millions. They are extraordinary little books, hand-written and hand-drawn in exquisite pen and ink. With echoes of Wordsworth's love affair with the Lakes, Wainwright, opens his very first book, *The Eastern Fells*, published in 1955, with these words of passion:

> Surely there is no other place in this whole wonder-
> ful world quite like Lakeland ... no other so exquisitely
> lovely, no other so charming, no other that calls so insis-
> tently across a gulf of distance. All who truly love Lakeland
> are exiles when they are away from it ...
>
> This book is one man's way of expressing his devo-
> tion to Lakeland's friendly hills. It was conceived and is
> born, after many years of inarticulate worshipping at their
> shrines.
>
> It is, in very truth, a love letter.

And then the introduction is followed by the reassuringly familiar format. Each fell, crag and pike is described and illustrated in alphabetical order beginning in this first book with Arnison Crag, less than a mile south of Patterdale. The detail, the clarity, the exactness given to each climb is incomparable.

* * *

Wainwright was born in Blackburn on 17 January 1907. He had an older brother and two older sisters. His father was a stonemason who drank a lot, spent much of his money on alcohol and was often unemployed. As a result the family lived in relative poverty in a small, two-bedroomed terraced house, no bathroom, and an outside toilet. It was Wainwright's mother who was the family rock. She was hard-working and in spite of a ne'er-do-well husband, she was keen to keep up a decent and respectable appearance.

Alfred was a bright boy. He shone at school. Nevertheless, and not unusual for the times, he left school at thirteen. However, whereas most of his classmates were destined to end up in the local cotton mills, Alfred got a job as an office boy in the local borough engineer's department. Thus began his life as a council employee. Night school led to qualifications in accountancy. His career path was set.

Wainwright's ethic of hard work, high standards and self-discipline made him intolerant of sloppiness and any hint of laziness. In his memoirs he feels that:

> People have lost satisfaction in doing a job well. ... We have to go back centuries in time to find the best architects, the best builders, the best painters, the best composers, the best sculptors; these men were infinitely superior. They had patience, skill and pride in their work. That's the difference between then and now.

Clearly not a fan of modernity.

Always a keen walker, he took his first trip, by bus, to the Lake District in 1930. He was aged twenty-three and the plan was to go on a week's walking holiday along with his cousin Eric Beardsall. They arrived in Windermere, left the bus station and climbed the nearest hill. Orrest Head, only half a mile north of Windermere, rises a modest 780 feet (238 metres), but it offers panoramic views across the lake and beyond to the Old Man of Coniston and the mountains of the central dome. Wainwright captures that moment of ecstasy that so many of us have experienced when we climb our first hill and gaze at the world around, above and below.

It was a moment of magic, a revelation so unexpected that I stood transfixed, unable to believe my eyes. I saw mountain ranges, one after another, the nearer starkly etched, those beyond fading into the blue distance. Rich woodlands, emerald pastures and the shimmering waters of the lake below added to the pageant of loveliness, a glorious panorama that held me enthralled. I had seen landscapes of rural beauty pictured in the local art gallery, but this was no painted canvas; this was real. This was truth. God was in his heaven that day and I a humble worshipper.

Those 'few hours on Orrest Head,' wrote Wainwright, 'changed my life.' Although Blackburn is only fifty miles from the Lake District, it was too far to satisfy Wainwright's hunger for the hills. So in 1941 he took a job, at lower pay, with Kendal borough treasurer's department. He had married his first wife, Ruth, a mill worker, in 1931 and together they had a son, Peter. The family headed north.

Valuing his meticulous and thorough ways, Kendal promoted him to borough treasurer in 1948, a post in which he remained until his retirement in 1967. Living and working in Kendal gave Wainwright the opportunity to walk and wander the fells much more intensively, at weekends, of an evening, during holidays. And then the idea came to him that to draw and write about his walks would be an added pleasure.

It was on 9 November 1952 that Alfred Wainwright, who preferred to be known as AW, began to write and draw the first of his guidebooks. He planned to write the seven guides over a thirteen-year period, and being Alfred that's exactly how long it took. 'The first page I did depicted the ascent of Dove Crag from Ambleside', although alphabetically it eventually appeared as his seventh walk. Being an absolute labour of love, the project became all consuming.

Partly to avoid other walkers, and partly to experience the mountains as the sun set and the sun rose, he began to spend nights on the fells. Although as a boy Wainwright's son, Peter, is present in quite a few of his father's photographs and drawings, more often than not Wainwright preferred walking on his own. He was famously antisocial, self-confessedly so as he admits in his memoir:

> It is the man or woman who walks alone who enjoys the greatest rewards, who sees and feels and senses the mood of the hills and knows them most intimately, and it is no coincidence that they are the people of abundant common sense and initiative and imagination. To the man in a conducted party the mountains are prose, to the man travelling alone they are poetry. Of course he has nobody to talk to, which is an advantage, and there is nobody to talk to him, which is a bigger advantage ... I always consider myself, when alone, a vastly entertaining companion, but when with others am considered unsociable, boorish, not with it.

And there is, of course, the story told by his second wife, Betty, when she asked if she could sometimes join him on his walks. 'Yes,' he replied, 'so long as you don't talk.' Wainwright certainly had obsessive traits. He liked routine. He insisted on watching *Coronation Street* every night. In contrast to his fell walking he lacked adventure in terms of food, preferring fish and chips whenever and wherever possible.

For the thirteen years of the project, nearly all of Wainwright's spare time was taken up with walking, writing and drawing. The meticulous pen-and-ink drawings are the guides' defining delight. They are beautiful; works of art. And they suggest the complex nature of the man's character. His exquisite, disciplined draftsmanship and obsession with detail and accuracy produce works of wonder and joy. Passion and perfection combine.

The mountains had an emotional pull on his life that he couldn't resist. And although he says that 'Lakeland is an emotion, and emotions are felt not expressed,' his guides belie this reticence. Every page is a 'love letter' to the lakes. 'Between finishing one book and starting the next,' he writes, 'I paused only to refill my pipe.'

Wainwright was quite apologetic about the fact that his intricate drawings were all based on the photographs he took. He felt he was 'cheating'. When a promising view appeared he would stop and take a photograph. He didn't take a sketchbook with him; 'a clear photograph' was enough. When he got home, he would take the photograph and use it to create his own, clear, sharp, beautifully interpreted drawing. In this translation from photograph to ink drawing, he ended up producing works of great clarity and charm. But in his memoir, he thinks:

> I was a cheapjack at the game. But I am sure fidelity to the scene has not suffered … the detail, and the relationship of one feature to all the rest, is foolproof. I wasn't aiming to be an artist, anyway. My aim was to draw mountains, not in a romantic and imaginative sense, but as they are. Yes, I was a fraud. With me, it was the result that mattered, not the means.

Wainwright was being unduly hard on himself. He wasn't a fraud. Ever since the invention of the camera, artists have used photographs to help them paint portraits, landscapes, seascapes and the sky. The art lies in the interpretation. The beauty is created out of the artist's experience of what they feel or see. In fact, the use of optical technology goes back many centuries.

Many great painters used the camera obscura – a lens that projected an inverted image onto a screen – in their work. In his book, *Secret Knowledge: Rediscovering the lost techniques of the Old Masters*, the artist David Hockney explores how artists such as Vermeer, and possibly Rembrandt, Velazquez, Caravaggio and others used mirrors and lenses to help them paint their portraits and capture their subject. The Pre-Raphaelite, Sir John Everett Millais often asked his friend, Rupert Potter, father of Beatrix Potter, to take photographs of the scenes or people he was painting so that when he was back in his studio he could use them as an aide-memoire. The simplicity and clarity that Wainwright wanted to achieve in his pen-and-ink drawings to guide the walker worked wonderfully well, but in the process he also managed to produce pictorial gems in pure black and white.

The seventh and final volume of his original Pictorial Guides, *The Western Fells*, was published in 1966. A year later, and only a few weeks before his retirement as Kendal borough treasurer in 1967, Ruth, his wife left him. It hadn't been a happy marriage. This was not to say that Wainwright wasn't a romantic soul. Clearly his emotional responses to the elements reveal the deeper currents of his passionate nature. These came to surface when he remarried again in 1970. His marriage to Betty was an altogether happier affair. In spite of his injunction not to talk too much, she often accompanied him on his trips. In his younger days Wainwright had used public transport, especially buses, to get around Lakeland. But in his later years Betty would drive them, not just around Cumbria, but to the Scottish Highlands, the Northern Pennines and the Yorkshire Dales.

Wainwright wrote *Memoirs of a Fellwanderer* when his fell wandering days were over. The first edition was published in 1993, not long after his death. He saw the book as 'a thanksgiving for the countless blessings' he had enjoyed throughout his lifetime. The book ends asking that his ashes be taken to one of his favourite spots, the little tarn tucked quietly beneath the slopes of Hay Stacks.

> All I ask for, at the end, is a last long resting place by the
> side of Innominate Tarn, on Haystacks. … A quiet place,
> a lonely place. I shall go to it, for the last time, and be
> carried: someone who knew me in life will take me and
> empty me out of a little box and leave me there alone.
> And if you, dear reader, should get a bit of grit in your
> boot as you are crossing Haystacks in the years to come,
> please treat it with respect. It might be me.

Alfred Wainwright died on 20 January 1991, aged eighty-four.
Betty, his wife, and Wainwright's old friend, Percy Duff and Percy's
two sons, Paul and Michael, did the honours. Peter and his father
were not particularly close and, by the time Wainwright died, Peter
was suffering with severe arthritis, all of which meant that he did not
join the group to scatter Wainwright's ashes. Betty wrote that on the
22 March 1991:

> We left Kendal at 6 am when it was still dark and we were
> near the summit of Haystacks just before 9 am. No one
> else was about. The day before had been sullen and wet
> and so was the day following, but that morning was per-
> fect. The sun rose steadily in a blue sky. I left him as he had
> requested, beside Innominate Tarn, and the larks sang a
> song of welcome.

Chapter 17

A FORCE OF NATURE

I am standing on the newly laid tarmac on the road looking up at the house in which Harriet Martineau lived for thirty years. My plan was to knock on the door and with huge apologies for the unannounced visit, say a quick hello and big thanks to one of the current owners, Barbara Todd, who had written a lovely little book about its original occupant, *Harriet Martineau at Ambleside with 'A Year at Ambleside'*. But I had learned earlier in the day that she was unwell. So instead, and at what I hope is a discreet distance, I gaze up at The Knoll, trying to imagine the redoubtable Miss Martineau marching down the garden steps, off into the village, to organise this and sort out that.

I admit I was rather selective in my choice of authors of Lakeland guides in the previous chapters. My defence is that their books have been among the more successful, their prose the most poetic. What also might have come through is that they were people of strong views which they were not afraid to voice. Wordsworth, Martineau and Wainwright rarely held back in what they thought and felt about people and places, especially as they related to the landscape of the Lakes.

Harriet Martineau, certainly, was regarded by all who ever met her as a force of nature, someone who provoked strong feelings, both for and against.

Harriet Martineau was born in Norwich on 12 June 1802 in the same house in which the Quaker and great social reformer Elizabeth

Fry had been born in 1780. She was the sixth child of eight. The family was reasonably prosperous. They were Unitarians, a practice that lent itself to fair play and dissenting views. However, Martineau described her mother as overbearing and her childhood as miserable. The wrongs she felt she suffered at the hands of her mother, brothers and sisters left her with 'a devouring passion for justice' which 'was precisely what was least understood in our house in regard to servants and children'.

Life became even more difficult for Harriet when, as a teenager, she began to go increasingly deaf. For most of her life she would use an ear trumpet. Reading became her solace. She was an avid reader of the news and throughout her life she was keen to keep up with events. She credits this early interest in news and finance with her later fame as a political economist and commentator.

After some schooling and a return to a dullish home life, she began to try her hand at writing. Her first article, 'Female Writers on Practical Divinity', was published in the Unitarian *Monthly Repository*. She wrote a second article 'On Female Education' in which she made a passionate appeal for the education of women. One of her older brothers was so impressed he wrote saying 'leave it to other women to make shirts and darn stockings and you devote yourself to this.' It was already becoming clear that Martineau was on her way to becoming a strong advocate of equality and justice, not just for women but for all those who suffered discrimination of one kind or another.

Although she never married, she did become engaged to John Hugh Worthington, a young Unitarian minister. However, not long after their announcement, John became ill and died in 1827. Although Martineau records her grief, she also expressed some relief that the relationship had ended albeit under sad circumstances. In her autobiography she writes, 'I am, in truth, very thankful for not having married at all. I have never since been tempted, nor have suffered any thing at all in relation to that matter which is held to be all-important to woman, – love and marriage'. She threw herself into her writing. Along with her 'political' pieces, she began to try her hand at writing short stories. And so bit by bit she found herself beginning to earn money from her pen.

By 1829, the family's fortunes suffered a major setback. Martineau moved to stay with her aunt and uncle in London. It was there that she began to mingle with many of the capital's radical intellectual and literary figures. Even after her mother insisted that she return home to Norwich, Martineau carried on writing. Her star continued to rise. She wrote for a general readership with pieces on politics, the economy and what today we would call sociological topics. She tackled the issue of slavery, the need for population control. Her output was prolific. Her monthly articles sold in their tens of thousands. She also had a go at writing short novels and edifying tales. 'Nobody is doing this country more good in England than this lady' said the *Spectator*. Coleridge, Darwin and the young princess, soon to be Queen Victoria, were said to be fans. By 1832 she was back in London mixing with the great and the good of the literary world. Such was her popularity that Queen Victoria invited Martineau to her coronation 1838.

In 1834 she sailed to America where she stayed a couple of years. She met President Jackson. True to her social reformist principles, Martineau publicly declared her support for those who wished to abolish slavery. On her return to England in 1836 she wrote *Society in America*, a three-volume book in which she railed against the inequalities suffered by both women and slaves. The emancipation of women became increasingly important to Martineau. Her radicalism earned her many admirers but it also created not a few enemies.

It was while she was in Venice on a short tour of Europe in 1839 that Martineau became very ill. The diagnosis was a uterine tumour. She returned home and moved up to Newcastle to stay with her sister Elizabeth whose husband, Thomas Greenhow, was a doctor. A year later she took lodgings in Tynemouth.

Although unwell and rarely leaving her rooms, she continued writing, not just essays, pamphlets and stories, but letters to friends and admirers. One of her earliest and life-long correspondents was Florence Nightingale. To ease her pains, Martineau began to take opiates. More drastically, she confined herself to her bed for the next five years. Even so, she managed to take advantage of her situation and wrote a series of bestselling essays that she called *Life in the Sickroom*. However, the essayist and philosopher Thomas Carlyle wasn't impressed. Aggressively he wrote, 'Harriet Martineau in her sick-room writes as if she were a female Christ, saying, "Look at me; see how I am suffering!"'

It was during her stay at Tynemouth that she came across the fashionable, somewhat controversial, treatment known as 'mesmerism'. It claimed to employ techniques that could shift the body's 'energy field' by inducing trance-like states in the patient. Austrian Franz Anton Mesmer, believed that a lack of balance in the magnetic-like fluid that ran through people's bodies could make them ill. To cure the patient, he or she was put into a trance-like, hypnotic state. The mesmerist then used strokes or 'passes' to interrupt the energy field, hoping to effect a cure.

Harriet Martineau invited the mesmerist Spencer Hall to treat her. After her first session she experienced a remarkable recovery. Further sessions, some even administered by her maid whom Martineau gave instructions on how to induce a trance, resulted in 'all pain and distress' giving way. She stopped taking the opiates. She became 'gay and talkative'. And, as if anticipating Carlyle's ridicule and scepticism, she announced that she felt 'resurrected!'. She took a final 'course' of mesmerism at the hands of a Mrs Wynyard and by the end of December 1844 she felt completely cured. And being Martineau, she immediately wrote about her experiences in 'Letters on Mesmerism' which were published in *The Athenaeum*, and then later as a popular pamphlet.

She began to take walks. Each day she took herself a little further. By early 1845 she felt fully recovered and decided that she needed a complete change of scene. She had had an invitation from friends in Windermere to visit. They lived at Wansfell Holme which lay on the southern outskirts of Ambleside overlooking the lake. This was Martineau's first visit to Lakeland and, like so many before and since, she fell in love with the place. Martineau decided there and then that this was where she wanted to live. She later wrote 'That month determined my place of residence for, probably, the rest of my life.'

It was while she was walking by the River Rothay beneath Loughrigg Fell that she looked across the fields and saw a knoll on rising ground. That was where, she decided, she would build her house. And indeed, that is where she did build her house, The Knoll, on Ambleside's northern fringes. It was designed to her own specifications and building started on 28 August 1845.

The speed with which The Knoll was built caused Mary Wordsworth, never the greatest admirer of Harriet's, to observe that Miss Martineau must have mesmerised her workmen. The house looked across the Rothay valley to Fox How, the home that had been built by Dr Thomas Arnold, headmaster of Rugby School. He built the house in 1833 as a summer holiday home and died there, of a heart attack, in 1842. His son, the poet Matthew Arnold, inherited Fox How, and it remained as a home and holiday destination for the family. Today the house is surrounded by trees and you'd be hard pressed to see it from The Knoll.

Among the many house-warming presents Martineau received was an ebony *papeterie* (a box for papers and writing materials) from Florence Nightingale. The diarist, lawyer and friend of many of the literary giants of the age, Henry Crabb Robinson, gave her a marble-topped sideboard which he had commissioned Mary Wordsworth to buy on his behalf.

Martineau was quick to make the acquaintance of the Wordsworths, who lived only a mile up the road at Rydal Mount. William was getting on a bit by now. He was in his mid-seventies. Nevertheless, he still fancied himself as a gardener and was still regarded as an authority on what to plant in the Lake District. Gardeners, like architects, he said, should let nature be their guide. He suggested that Martineau plant a couple of stone pines to commemorate her new life. He even helped plant one of them himself. Given their provenance, Martineau was desperate to keep them healthy, but in the event only one survived.

William and Dorothy Wordsworth were happy to invite their famous new neighbour over for tea and chats, especially of an evening. But Martineau preferred to visit in daylight rather than dark. However, it wasn't her eyesight that was the problem but her deafness. In the evening the elderly William would remove his false teeth. The result was that his words became mumbly and less distinct. Martineau had a job understanding what he was saying, so she kept her visits to daylight hours and a fully dentured Wordsworth.

There were many topics about which the conservative William and the radical Martineau were bound to disagree. Martineau was a radical and a humanist who welcomed change, both political and economic. She was at heart a rationalist who believed that men and women, through reason, could create a better world. This was in spite of her conviction that the mystical mesmerism had cured her pains. Wordsworth did not believe in her mesmerism, but he did enjoy her enthusiasm and vitality. He was certainly impressed with her capacity for taking long, challenging walks. They developed a friendship of sorts by not talking about politics or any of the controversial issues of the day. However, Mary Wordsworth was not so easily won over. She tried to avoid Martineau's unannounced visits by slipping out for a walk every afternoon around two o'clock.

In spite of her delight with her new home, in late 1846 Martineau left for a tour of the Middle East. She returned to Ambleside in October 1847, and the first thing she did was write a book about her experiences. *Eastern Life, Past and Present* was published in 1848. It was an ambitious project. She examined the origins of the old Abrahamic faiths of Judaism, Christianity and Mohammedism as well as the faith of the ancient Egyptians. What she identified was a trend that started with a belief in many gods, then the notion of a holy trinity, before finally the idea of a single deity. Although she had retained the radicalism of her Unitarian upbringing, she had lost much of her traditional faith. Her studies led her to a kind of philosophical atheism. Unsurprisingly she was heavily criticised by many high church, conservative Victorians. Douglas Jerrold, a writer and dramatist, cuttingly said 'There is no God, and Harriet Martineau is His Prophet'.

Back home in Ambleside, Martineau threw herself into local life. Now in her early forties, she took to the hills and, in her own words, a life of 'wild roving'. She particularly enjoyed the Lakes in winter when there were fewer tourists and even fewer fans, who took it upon themselves to wander into her garden and gawp through her windows.

She liked stormy days. In her little book *A Year at Ambleside*, which described village life month by month, she said, 'To struggle on against wind and splashing rain, in a thoroughly waterproof dress, is really pleasurable when it happens in the morning, when one has no fear of being benighted, when one is unfatigued and going home to breakfast by a bright fireside.' The joy she experienced, whatever the weather threw at her, marked the beginning of her life as a committed Lakelander.

But true to her progressive ideas, she also welcomed change. Although she had only just arrived in the area, in 1845 she attended the opening ceremony to mark the start of a new service being offered on Windermere. *Lady of the Lake* was the first paddle steamship to operate on an English lake (a different *Lady of the Lake* to Ullswater's 1877 craft). Needless to say, Wordsworth refused to attend, fearing yet more tourists wandering the valleys, picking the daffodils and disturbing the peace.

In 1848 Martineau began to give regular lectures in Ambleside to working men and women. She discoursed on topics of every kind – on politics, communal home building, hygiene, the history of England, temperance, and the effects of alcohol on the brain and stomach.

With her strong views on social justice and equality she also decided to practise what she preached. In 1849, she got a group of fellow-minded reformers together to form The Windermere Permanent Land, Building, and Investment Association to build better quality houses for the poor and elderly. She was bothered by the lack of good quality homes for the labourers and workers who lived in small, cheaply built cottages, often sleeping ten to twelve in just two rooms Their plight was brought into even sharper relief by the growing number of grand houses being built locally by wealthy factory owners from Lancashire. Where Wordsworth saw the ideal cottage growing organically out of its native rock, the socialist Martineau saw slum dwellings unfit for human habitation. She set about raising money, talked about the principles of a building society and buying houses, bought some land, and with her supporters set about building a dozen or more good quality grey-stone wall cottages in Ambleside on Ellerigg Road which are still there to this day.

On 16 December 1849 a young novelist came to stay at The Knoll. Martineau had met her a year earlier in London. The young woman was Charlotte Brontë. Even before Martineau had realised who the woman was, she told Brontë (who was still writing under the name of Currer Bell at the time) that she thought the novel, *Jane Eyre*, was 'first rate'. Praise from Martineau, who was older and better known at the time, went down well with Charlotte, who naturally thought Martineau a splendid person. 'She seems to me the benefactress of Ambleside' wrote Brontë, 'yet takes no sort of credit to herself for active and indefatigable philanthropy ... her servant and her poor neighbours love as well as respect her.' True, Brontë also thought that Martineau was 'not without peculiarities, but I have seen none as yet which annoy me. She is both hard and warm-hearted, abrupt and affectionate, liberal and despotic.'

After Brontë's stay at The Knoll, the two writers remained in contact for a while but their relationship, at least as far as Brontë was concerned, was destined to take a turn for the worse. As a friend and fellow writer, Brontë asked Martineau to give her candid opinion on *Villette*, a new novel still in draft. Martineau, being the woman she was, took Brontë at her word. She gave her candid opinion.

In her efforts to be critically constructive, Martineau was her usual straight, direct, tell-it-like-it-is self. She wrote back saying that she felt some of the more emotionally passionate sections of the book were not working for her. The feedback upset and angered Brontë. She vowed never to visit Ambleside again. However, Martineau, innocent of Brontë's hurt feelings, still invited the young novelist back to The Knoll. But only a few years after their first meeting, Brontë died. She was thirty-eight, and pregnant. Still unaware of Brontë's umbrage, Martineau wrote an obituary in *The Daily News* sincerely praising Brontë's considerable talents. Brontë would not have been the first, nor indeed the last, to feel a bit rocked by her encounter with Martineau, but the older woman always meant well.

Martineau's appetite for life led to the purchase of two and a half acres of land adjacent to The Knoll. She wanted to extend her garden and do a spot of farming. She bought two cows. The local belief was that two cows would need much more than two acres if they were going to thrive. Martineau decided to challenge Westmorland wisdom and Cumberland tradition that believed one cow needed three acres of grass to milk well. She also bought pigs and poultry. A vegetable garden was dug. To run the little smallholding Martineau invited a labourer from Norfolk to join her in Ambleside. The venture was a success. Her experimental method of farming caused much local, indeed national, interest. And what did she do? Well, she did what she always did. She wrote up her 'methods' in a pamphlet: *Health, Husbandry and Handicraft*.

Martineau was keen to impress anyone who might show an interest in her farming innovations. During one of Matthew Arnold's visits to Fox How, Harriett decided to invite him to admire her bovine beauties. He later recalled the invitation saying that while he had been talking 'to Miss Martineau (who blasphemes frightfully) about the prospects of the Church of England, and, wretched man that I am, promised to go and see her cow-keeping miracles tomorrow – I, who hardly know a cow from a sheep.'

During her literary life Martineau wrote 1,640 articles for *The Daily News* (a left-leaning paper founded, and initially edited, by Charles Dickens). The subjects she tackled included the American Revolution, agricultural labour, drainage, irrigation in the East and 'India for the Indians'. She wrote other pieces for Dickens when he became editor of a weekly magazine, *Household Words*, first published in 1850 before it finally ended its run in 1859.

And in the middle of all this bustle and activity she somehow found time to translate and condense Augustus Comte's classic and highly influential pioneering books on sociology *Philosophie Positive,* which were written between 1830 and 1842. These highly technical books were not easy reads, in English never mind French. But she admirably captured his main ideas and rendered them accessible for both professional and lay audiences alike. His chunky six books were boiled down into two manageable volumes that Martineau titled *The Positive Philosophy of Auguste Comte.* They were published in 1853 and greatly admired as works of considerable scholarship.

* * *

In early 1855, Martineau began to feel unwell. Accompanied by her maid, she visited London and saw Dr Peter Mere Latham. He diagnosed a heart condition and a large abdominal tumour. Martineau was convinced she didn't have long to live so she began to write her autobiography. However, although her health did gradually deteriorate, and although she did put on a lot of weight, it would be another twenty-one years before she died.

Martineau died in the evening of 27 June 1876. The post-mortem confirmed the presence of the fatal tumour. The abdominal tumour that she thought had been cured by mesmerism had never really gone away. She was finally buried next to her mother in a cemetery in Birmingham.

Her time in Cumbria brought her much contentment. She was certainly a significant presence, locally in terms of her involvement with all kinds of people and projects, and nationally in terms of her vast, often controversial writing output. If you stroll through Ambleside along the A591 towards Rydal, on the wall of the hall where she gave her village lectures there is a blue, oval plaque which records that Harriet Martineau, writer and reformer 'Lectured Here'.

* * *

Today, there is a revival of interest in the life and writings of Harriet Martineau. She is seen by many, including Anthony Giddens, emeritus professor of sociology at the LSE, as the first female sociologist, indeed one of the founders of the discipline itself. Her biographer, Shelagh Hunter wrote that Martineau 'anticipated feminism in her life as she did sociology in her thought'. Her politics remained radical. She was an early and staunch advocate of women's emancipation. Every inch of her life was a rebuke to those who believed that women were not capable of original thought, hard work, strong views and endless stamina. She is also the subject of an annual lecture – The Harriet Martineau Lecture – which was given by the author Ali Smith in 2013, the writer Kate Mosse in 2014, the reggae poet Linton Kwesi Johnson in 2016 in recognition of Martineau's progressive campaigning on behalf of black emancipation, and Mexican journalists Lydia Cacho and Anabel Hernández in 2017 describing their international campaign to lay bare the corruption and violence of their government. By anybody's reckoning Martineau was an extraordinary woman.

She said her happiest days were those in which she had lived and worked in the Lake District. Although they only overlapped by a few years, the presence of two of the literary giants of their day, Miss Harriet Martineau and Mr William Wordsworth, does seem quite an achievement for such a small town tucked away among the fells of the far north-west. But it is yet another reminder of the power of the Lake District to attract strong minds, inspire romantic souls, nurture creative spirits and fire the imagination. The inhabitants of Ambleside were left in no doubt that in Martineau, a phenomenon had arrived in their midst. And as if to seal her legend, towards the end of her life she even took up cigarette and cigar smoking.

To end this particular story, this is how John Cranstoun Nevill sums up Martineau's astonishing life:

Of her capacity there can be no question: she was full of engaging little idiosyncrasies ... she had more than her fair share of moral arrogance inherent in most Victorians, and she could, at times, be narrow and absurdly prejudiced in her attitude toward life; but, like a rock embedded in a superficially changeful sea, the basic mind was there – strong, fearless and, in effect, inflexible ... She was among the first of those nineteenth-century pioneers – Elizabeth Fry, Charlotte Brontë, Florence Nightingale, George Eliot – to mention only a few at random – who by sheer force of character broke through the male police cordon which excluded their sex from any active participation in public affairs, so that there is hardly an intellectual freedom enjoyed by the women of today that does not give back some far-off lingering re-echo of her voice.

Spot on.

Chapter 18

BACK TO NATURE

Landscapes of grandeur and beauty do, it seems, attract minds of a certain character. Romantics, certainly. By the end of the eighteenth century, painters as well as poets began to find inspiration among the hills and by the waters of the Lake District. J.M.W. Turner made several visits including one in 1816, 'the year without summer' when skies world-wide remained yellow and dusty with ash as a result of the violent eruption of the Indonesian volcano, Mount Tambora, the previous year. John Constable's sketches and paintings based on his 1806 trip to the Lakes are softer and more gentle in style than those of Turner but equally evocative. There are twentieth and twenty-first century artists, too, who have experienced and interpreted the Lakes in ways that give us a deep emotional feel for the life and landscape of Cumbria. Sheila Fell was one such artist. She was born in Aspatria, Cumberland on 20 July 1931. Although she lived and worked for much of her life in London, the Lake District remained her main theme and influence. She was befriended by L. S. Lowry, who also bought many of her pictures. Fell's paintings of hills and houses are densely textured, restless and often brooding. There is an expressionistic, van Gogh-like quality to her work. She died in 1979, aged only forty-eight.

As well as the poets and painters, there are also lovers of nature whose views easily slip into environmentalism. There are environmentalists who have conservational, indeed conservative tendencies.

They morph into traditionalists and worry that the ancient beauty of the Lakes might be destroyed by the vulgar and new.

John Ruskin, a poet, artist, art critic, philosopher, conservationist, scientist, writer of beautiful prose and all-round polymath, was firmly in the traditionalist camp. In the final third of his life, he was drawn to the Lake District where he eventually set up home.

John Ruskin was the only child of prosperous parents. He was born in London on 8 February 1819. His father traded in wine and sherry, a business that required him to travel extensively in both Europe and Britain. John would often accompany his father on these trips. He fell in love with the Alps and many of Europe's grander cities. But his journeys around Britain probably influenced his later life even more. In his dealings with the rich and privileged, his father visited many of the island's great country houses. Even before he went off to university, Ruskin had travelled through much of Scotland and the wealthy shires of England. On their annual visit to stay with an aunt in Perth, the family often stopped off in the Lake District and took a holiday.

Although their lives overlapped by a number of years, Ruskin only saw Wordsworth on two occasions. The first time was when Ruskin and his parents were on one of their Lake District holidays. On Sunday, 4 July 1830, the Ruskin family attended the service at St Mary's church, Rydal. Wordsworth was also present, but he failed to make a strong impression on the eleven-year-old boy. The young Ruskin noted that the sixty-year-old poet, with his long face and large nose, seemed to sleep throughout most of the service. In contrast, Robert Southey, who was also present, remained awake and, at least to Ruskin's delicate eye, looked more like a poet ought to look.

The young John became inspired by whatever he saw — landscapes, architecture, paintings. As a teenager, he showed a precocious talent as an artist. He wrote poems. He drew maps. His first poem to be published, 'On Skiddaw and Derwent Water', appeared in 1830 when he was only twelve. It was printed in the *Spiritual Times*.

In his early years John was educated at home by tutors as well as by his parents, both of whom had lofty ambitions for their son. When he was in his mid-teens, he spent a year at a school run by the progressive evangelist, Thomas Dale. In 1836 Ruskin went up to the University of Oxford. He read Latin and Greek. He attended lectures given by the geologist, William Buckland. He was writing more poetry. Indeed, it was Ruskin's prowess as a poet that led to his second and final meeting with William Wordsworth. On 12 June 1839 Wordsworth was being awarded with his honorary Doctor of Civil Law degree from the University of Oxford. Ruskin the under-graduate was also being recognised. He had won the Newdigate Prize for his poem 'Salsette and Elephanta'. Dressed in his new doc-toral robes, it was the sixty-nine-year-old Wordsworth who handed the prize to Ruskin, who was then asked to read out loud his poem. However, Ruskin's health at this time was not good and for a while he took a break from his studies. He eventually graduated in 1842.

One of Ruskin's unusual strengths was to see and sense nature in all its detail. He was a great observer of all things natural – plants, rocks, weather. Even in his teens he had written observational papers for the *Magazine of Natural History*. Ruskin recognised that curiosity could lead to scientific wonder as well as poetic beauty. Although Ruskin generally admired Wordsworth, and like him believed that a love of nature ennobled men and women, unlike the poet he under-stood that 'to break a rock with a hammer in search of a crystal may sometimes be an act not disgraceful to human nature, and that to dissect a flower may sometimes be as proper as to dream over it.'

Ruskin's essays, 'The Poetry of Architecture', were serialised in the *Architectural Magazine* during the months of 1837 and 1838. These papers were inspired by Wordsworth's strong belief that buildings should be sympathetic to their natural surroundings. Choice of stone, colour, scale and design should all ensure that buildings look and feel part of the natural landscape.

By his mid-twenties Ruskin began to write about painters and their art, especially landscape painters. He was particularly taken with Turner.

The 3rd Earl of Egremont held the Cumbrian seat of Cocker-mouth. He was not only a friend to Turner but also his patron. The artist first visited the Lake District in 1797. On many of his trips he would stay with the earl, whose home was Cockermouth Castle. Among Turner's many paintings of the district are scenes of Derwent Water, Coniston Water, Buttermere and Ullswater. Perhaps more than any other artist, Turner captures the natural power and restless energy of the lakes, mountains and the brooding skies. *Buttermere Lake, with Part of Cromackwater, Cumberland, a Shower* is one particular painting that arose out of Turner's Lakeland tours. Its black waters, rain swept skies and arching rainbow of pure light was painted in 1798 and now hangs in Tate Britain, London. Turner's reputation as the painter who reveals the Lake District and its elemental power better than any other continues to stand the test of time. In his 1983 book, *Land of the Lakes*, Melvyn Bragg writes:

> Turner did the greatest paintings of the Lakes. 'Morning Amongst the Coniston Fells' and his dark study of Scafell stand as supreme among all other paintings as Wordsworth's poetry stands among other poets.

Ruskin's book *Modern Painters* was published in 1843. Just as buildings should be in harmony with their surroundings, so Ruskin also thought that landscape art should capture the truth and inherent beauty of nature. Paul Klee wrote that 'art does not reproduce the visible: rather, it makes it visible'. Ruskin criticised the contrived, artificial, studio-fabricated painters of earlier generations. Artists who, first hand, saw, felt, smelled, heard and tasted the rivers and rocks, wind and sky, fields and trees, light and sound, produced works of greater truth and deeper understanding. They explored the essence of things. Their work was visceral. There was passion. They could stir the emotions. Little wonder that he admired Turner so much.

Ruskin's books and essays began to redefine how nature was to be approached and viewed. He mixed aesthetics with science, observation with ethics, criticism with polemics. His path in life was set. And he was still only in his twenties.

He continued to travel around Europe, taking in the mountains and lakes, cities and buildings, painters and their art, both old and new. More essays and books on painting and architecture appeared. His arguments that beauty, imagination and the divine spirit went hand in hand became clearer and sharper. Ruskin's 'naturalism', seen in his own detailed watercolours and drawings slowly began to influence the artists of his day including the Pre-Raphaelites.

In 1848 Ruskin married Euphemia (Effie) Gray. She was the daughter of friends of the family with whom they stayed when up in Scotland. But the marriage was never consummated and was eventually annulled in 1854. Historians have had a great fun speculating why Ruskin never got around to having a sexual relationship with his wife.

In the summer of 1853, before the annulment, Ruskin invited the Pre-Raphaelite artist John Everett Millais to join him and Effie on a visit to Scotland. Effie had already posed for one of Millais' earlier paintings, *The Order of Release 1746*. Being an admirer of Millais' work, Ruskin asked the artist to paint a portrait of him. On their arrival in Scotland work on the painting began almost immediately.

Millais thought Ruskin a rather controlling client, one who wished to direct much of the creative process. The result, however, was what perhaps is the best-known portrait of John Ruskin. He is shown standing in front of a tumbling mountain stream. He is surrounded by rough rocks and cascading waters. The portrait is true to Ruskin's own philosophy that artists should 'go to nature in all singleness of heart'. However, on this particular occasion the artist not only went to nature with singleness of heart, his passions also took him to Effie. They fell in love and began an affair. After her eventual separation from Ruskin, in 1855 Effie married Millais. This marriage was consummated. The couple ended up producing eight children.

As the years went by, Ruskin felt more and more strongly that modern industrial practices, the de-skilling of labour, the greed of capitalism and the crude pursuit of wealth were corrupting people and their society. He celebrated craftsmanship. He thought highly of those who worked intimately with stone, wood, metal and fabric. Their knowledge of the natural and raw meant that they could create works that remained true to the materials with which they toiled. His ideas became the seeds of the Arts and Crafts Movement, soon to be sown and reaped to such great effect by William Morris.

Ruskin's interest in education began in the 1850s. He taught drawing. He lectured on architecture, painting, art, morals, philosophy, geology and botany. In 1869 he was appointed the first Slade professor of fine art at the University of Oxford. He believed that a good education should mix traditional subjects with dancing and sport, music and crafts.

His aesthetic beliefs also began to influence his social and political ideas. His hostility towards capitalism and its relentless drive to divide and de-skill labour increased. Working men and women were finding it more and more difficult to find dignity in their work. Craft was giving way to task, the artisan was being replaced by the factory worker. And with the fragmentation of the processes of production in which the worker became separated from the products of his labour came the fragmentation of the community. In Ruskin's eyes, capitalism was leading to the breakdown of social ties, co-operative endeavour, shared lives and a sense of belonging. None of this thinking went down particularly well with the industrialists and their conservative supporters. Ruskin's ideas appeared to hark back to an imagined age of happy peasants and rural idylls.

However, Ruskin did not believe in social equality. Some men, he thought, were naturally 'superior' to others in terms of wisdom and intellect. Such men – and it was mainly men he had in mind – were the natural leaders. They were the ones to guide, decide and orchestrate the lives of others, for the common good and social justice. Women did have important roles to play but they were confined to the home, education and the raising of children. Harriet Martineau would definitely not have agreed with Ruskin's politics and, indeed, by the end of the nineteenth century his patronising stance towards women was not going down well with the growing number of people who were pushing for fundamental improvements in the rights of women.

Ruskin's communitarian vision saw the return of craft skills, traditional farming techniques and old social hierarchies. The dignity to be found in making things, growing food and working co-operatively was an attractive prospect to many. It seemed a good way to fight the alienation that seemed endemic to modern industrial practices. If men and women were to be creative and content, then there must be a return to wholesome practices in which hands and minds, craftsmen and farmers, leaders and led, worked harmoniously together.

In the fourth volume of his book *Modern Painters*, published in 1856, Ruskin began to develop the idea that landscapes of great beauty and grandeur, such as the Alps, could affect the moral and spiritual character of those who lived beneath the mountains and by the rivers. It seemed only a matter time, therefore, before Ruskin would be drawn back to the Lake District. In the event, fifteen years passed.

His father died in 1864 leaving Ruskin a considerable fortune. In 1871 he bought Brantwood, a rather run-down house on the eastern shores of Coniston Water, which the money allowed him to modernise. Rooms were added. He was also keen to try out and realise many of his ideas. He built an ice house so that food could be kept cool in the summer. Like Wordsworth, Ruskin was keen to establish a garden according to his own design. A waterfall was redirected to tumble down the hillside. And on the shores of Coniston Water itself, he enlarged the moorings where he tied up his little rowing boat, *Jumping Jenny*. It was at Brantwood, in the Lake District, that Ruskin spent the last twenty-nine years of his life.

Towards the end of the century, Ruskin's views and ideas gradually began to fall out of fashion. The idea of 'art for art's sake', the rise of the Impressionists, and the relentless advance and intrusion of industry into every corner of life were not to his taste. And unlike Harriet Martineau, he was not happy with the ideas of Darwin, although he quite liked the man himself. Brantwood and the surrounding lakes and fells gradually began to fill more and more of his life. His last major work was his autobiography: *Praeterita,* that is to say 'Of Past Things', the first of the three volumes being published in 1885.

In his later years Ruskin's feudal outlook, obsessive tendencies and even his paranoid delusions became more pronounced. In January 1900 he fell ill with influenza. By the twentieth of that month he was dead, aged eighty. He is buried in at St Andrew's Church, Coniston. Above his tomb stands a tall Anglo-Saxon cross, ornately carved out of local green slate. He would have been pleased with that.

* * *

Since his death, Ruskin's reputation has not only recovered but also grown. Like Wordsworth, he seemed to anticipate the growing worries about the environmental damage caused by factory smoke and industrial pollution. In his lecture, 'The Storm-Cloud of the Nineteenth Century', delivered in 1884, he felt that human progress would foul the world leaving nothing but a 'blanched sun' and 'blighted grass'. Although the word 'ecology' was not yet in common usage, these romantic Lakelanders and their understanding of men and women's intimate relationship with nature made them ecological pioneers. When men and women set themselves apart from, and above nature, they break that organic unity that keeps the world in harmony and balance. Hubris is invariably followed by nemesis. We disregard our relationship with the vast interconnectedness of the natural world, say the ecologists, at our peril. We need, in the words of Jonathan Bate, an 'ecological consciousness.'

Architects, including Le Corbusier and Frank Lloyd Wright took note of Ruskin's views of form, function and beauty. Buildings, thought Ruskin, should be an expression in stone of truth, values and feeling. He wrote eloquently on the virtues and emotional strength of the Gothic. He lauded the skills of the medieval masons as they worked the stone with love and imagination. William Morris and the Arts and Crafts Movement acknowledged their debt to Ruskin. Those with utopian ambitions hoped that children might be educated, not just in reading, writing and arithmetic, but also in the arts and the crafts, body as well as mind. When men and women were allowed to put their hearts and souls into their work, they could become whole again, no longer cogs in the industrial machine.

When two American philanthropists were looking for a name to grace the new college they had founded in Oxford in 1899, Ruskin came to mind. Today, Ruskin College, Oxford, specialises in providing a higher educational experience to working men and women who had missed out on gaining qualifications during their school years. In effect, the college offers a 'second chance' to those who, through disadvantage or deprivation, never had the opportunity to realise their potential. The ethos and philosophy that underlies the educational experience is one that encourages social understanding and change.

John Ruskin's name also appears in the title of another place of higher learning. The Cambridge College of Art's inaugural lecture was given by Ruskin back in 1858. Over the years, the college evolved first into a polytechnic and then a university. Finally, in 2005, Anglia Polytechnic University was renamed Anglia Ruskin University in recognition of Ruskin's original support of the city's old art's college.

During his stay at Brantwood, Ruskin filled the house with paintings, minerals and crystals. In the early days, Brantwood was a busy place. Friends visited and stayed. Lessons were taught. The artist Arthur Severn and his family moved in to live with the great man. As Ruskin's health, both physical and mental, began to deteriorate he was cared for by Joan, Severn's wife who was also Ruskin's cousin. After his death in 1900, she inherited the house and its extensive grounds. The Severn family sold Brantwood and the surrounding estate in 1931. The house and lands were eventually bought by John Whitehouse and the Birmingham Ruskin Society. In 1951, Whitehouse established the Brantwood Trust.

Brantwood, its beautiful gardens and estate, are now open to the public. Many of Ruskin's designs, drawing and artefacts are displayed around the house. Programmes of art and craft exhibitions run throughout the year. You can even get married there, hopefully with happier results than Ruskin's own unconsummated marriage to Effie Gray.

Some of Ruskin's most influential legacies were his views on conservation and landscape. He feared that the purity of the natural landscape was being polluted by industry and commerce, chemicals and smoke, mechanisation and technology. He held a profound distaste for the growing cities and their ugly factories. In his 1860 essays, published as *Unto This Last*, Ruskin rails against the social wrongs of capitalism and anticipates many of the arguments later to be made the Green Movement. Industry's greed and rapacious disregard for the damage it inflicts on the natural world distressed him:

All England may, if it so chooses, become one manufacturing town; and Englishmen, sacrificing themselves to the good of general humanity, may live diminished lives in the midst of noise, of darkness, and of deadly exhalation. But the world cannot become a factory nor a mine. No amount of ingenuity will ever make iron digestible by the million, nor substitute hydrogen for wine. Neither the avarice nor the rage of men will ever feed them.

In Ruskin's world view, people would live contentedly, knowing their place in the social order as they ploughed the fields, milked their cows, spun yarn, forged iron and worked wood. Ruskin's views were those of a poet and a conservationist. He valued the song of a bird, the burble of a brook, the beauty of a tiny flower. Strands of his thinking became part of the early fabric that would eventually lead to the foundation of the National Trust. He appreciated open spaces, natural landscapes, sympathetic buildings and traditional farming.

Like Wordsworth, Ruskin fought plans to bring the railways into the central Lakes. In a letter to the *Pall Mall Gazette*, he wrote that the railways were 'the loathsomest form of devilry now extant ...

destructive of all wise social habitat or possible natural beauty.' The glory of the Lakes was in danger of being spoiled by 'the stupid herds of modern tourists'.

However, although the railways never made it into the heart of the Lakes, roads were improved and soon found their way along the valleys and between the hills. The years immediately after Ruskin's death marked the beginning of cheap, mass-produced cars. A day trip to the Lakes from the industrial cities of the North quickly became a possibility for more and more people. There was no denying that the steady decline of the region's mining industry, closure of the mills and the limited fortunes of hill-farming, meant that the most valuable asset that the Lake District could trade on was its remarkable scenery of mountains, rivers and lakes.

Chapter 19

HEDGEHOGS AND HERDWICKS

Someone else who would come to share many of Ruskin's views was Beatrix Potter. She had actually seen Ruskin in 1884 when she was seventeen. She was on a visit to the Royal Academy of Arts in Piccadilly. He was visiting too. They didn't meet, but the young Beatrix did observe the great man and wasn't terribly impressed.

'Mr Ruskin was one of the most ridiculous figures I have seen,' she wrote in her journal. He was wearing an old hat, an old coat, and one of his trouser legs was half tucked into to the top of his boots. 'He became aware of this half way round the room, and stood on one leg to put it right, but in doing so hitched up the other trouser worse than the first one had been.'

Helen Beatrix Potter was born in London on 28 July 1866. She had a younger brother, Bertram. Her father, Rupert Potter, was a barrister, and although he enjoyed some early success, he became less committed to his profession as he got older. On the death of his father he inherited much of the family's fortune. The money allowed him to pursue his hobbies. These included photography, drawing and an interest in art. When Rupert was a boy, the family were still living in the Manchester area. When he was sixteen, he attended the Unitarian Manchester College where he was taught by, indeed inspired by James Martineau, Harriet Martineau's younger brother.

Rupert had a modest talent for sketching and drawing. As a young man he had drawn a picture of ducks in flight, two of which wore bonnets tied with a ribbon under their chins. Beatrix kept these drawings. Twenty year later she would be drawing her own bonneted Jemima Puddle-duck.

One of Rupert Potter's friends was the painter John Everett Millais and his wife, Effie, of whom we heard in the last chapter. Beatrix often accompanied her father when he paid visits to Millais. The artist took an avuncular interest in some of young Beatrix's early drawings, while she thought his early paintings were wonderful.

Home life for the young Beatrix was gloomy, stuffy and rather lonely, at least until her brother came along six years later, although he was packed off to boarding school when he was old enough. Her mother had social pretensions and enjoyed mixing with other monied and genteel families.

Beatrix was schooled at home. Without friends and playmates, she learnt to entertain herself. 'Self-containment,' writes her biographer Matthew Dennison, 'was an important facet of her make-up. It surfaces in her fictional characters: Jeremy Fisher, Mrs Tiggy-winkle, Mrs Tittlemouse. All live apparently fulfilled, largely solitary lives.' However, in fairness to her father, he not only recognised his daughter's talents as an artist, he encouraged her skills and interests. He bought Beatrix books on art. He took her to see exhibitions. He arranged lessons for her. She went with him to visit Millais. Rupert would later express great pride in Beatrix's success as a writer and illustrator of children's books.

The sense of being a neglected child, one who became increasingly exasperated with her own parents, later manifests itself in Beatrix's stories. Matthew Dennison observes how many of Beatrix's tales feature incomplete families and poor parenting. Peter Rabbit, Tom Kitten and Pigling Bland don't have a father. Jemima Puddle-duck is a hopeless mother. Tabitha Twitchit is an 'anxious parent' who swings helplessly between attempts at discipline and feeling out of control.

From a young age Beatrix began to draw. It became a compulsion. 'I cannot rest. I must draw, however poor the result,' the eighteen-year-old wrote in her journal, October 1884. Although home-life lacked friends, it did not lack books, art and most importantly wild-life. Throughout her childhood Beatrix had kept animals of all kinds – dogs, mice, a rat, a hedgehog, guinea pigs, a tortoise, caged birds, bats, lizards, newts, a frog, snails, caterpillars, a duck and rabbits. All were given names, all offered the lonely Beatrix companionship, and most were drawn.

Like Harriet Martineau, Beatrix was raised as a Unitarian. It was a dissenting faith. Jesus was not seen as divine but rather as a human intermediary between God and man. It helped foster a strong sense of self-reliance in Beatrix. The faith also encouraged, as it did in Martineau, a rationalist, scientific outlook on all things, social as well as natural. This would become evident in Beatrix's extremely detailed and methodical observations and drawings of the natural world – plants, flowers, animals, fossils.

Unitarianism also encouraged an emphasis on social responsibil-ity, although this was not strongly evident in Beatrix's own parents. Her paternal grandfather, Edmund Potter, whom Beatrix was said to resemble, was not only artistic and intellectually curious, he was a highly successful businessman. His Glossop-based cotton and calico printing factories made him and her father's family very rich.

Edmund became a significant figure in Manchester's business world, and true to his Unitarian values he involved himself in the city's social and philanthropic life too. In further recognition of his innovative work in calico printing, in 1855 he was elected President of the Manchester School of Art, a post he held for three years before eventually becoming Liberal Member of Parliament for Carlisle. He also bought a country estate of over 300 acres in Hertfordshire, a place that Beatrix grew to love as a child.

Holidays for Beatrix's family were regular and frequent, taking up to four months out of most years. The Potters holidayed in the West Country, Scotland and the Lake District. In the summer of 1882, when Beatrix was sixteen years old, the family stayed at Wray Castle on the western shores of Windermere. Holidays involved the whole household decamping from London. Staff, carriages, horses, even pets all made their way north to join the family.

* * *

The neo-Gothic Wray 'Castle', with its exaggerated turrets and crenellations, was built in 1840 by the retired Liverpool surgeon, James Dawson. However, it was not the castle that won Beatrix's heart but the countryside around of lakes and hills, rivers and woods. Upon his death, Dr Dawson had left Wray Castle to his nephew Edward Preston Rawnsley. He in turn invited his cousin, the Reverend Hardwicke Rawnsley, to become the vicar of the nearby church of St Margaret. The offer was made in 1877 and by early 1878 Rawnsley had settled in his new post. As well as being a clergyman, the Reverend Hardwicke Rawnsley was a poet, supporter of traditional skills and crafts, and keen conservationist.

It was while he had been at Oxford that he had come under the influence of John Ruskin, so much so that, aged twenty-six, he had no hesitation accepting his cousin's invitation to move to the Lake District to become the vicar of Wray, only five miles north-east of Brantwood, Ruskin's home.

In time Hardwicke Rawnsley would become the owner of Greta Hall, one-time home of both Coleridge and Southey. Later still, in 1915, he moved again and bought Allan Bank in Grasmere, one-time home of Wordsworth. In 1920, only three years after this final move, Rawnsley died. He is perhaps best remembered as being a key figure in founding The National Trust.

It was during the Potter family holidays in the Lake District that Beatrix met the charismatic Reverend Rawnsley. It was her meetings with, and encouragement by him that first gave Potter the idea that she could become a writer as well as illustrator of children's stories. Aged twenty-four, she already had had some success getting a number of her animal-themed pictures printed as Christmas and New Year cards. However, it was Beatrix's former governess, Annie Moore, who suggested that some of her ex-pupil's little stories might actually be worthy of publication.

Potter had been in the habit of writing to Annie's young children. She illustrated her letters and the stories she sent them with pictures of the animals she had written about. Indeed, Peter Rabbit made his very first appearance in one of these letters. Beatrix took up the suggestion and explored whether she might get the little stories published. But like so many writers down the ages, publisher after publisher rejected her submissions. It was at this point that Hardwicke Rawnsley once more intervened. He said he would help Beatrix resubmit the manuscript to the publisher, Frederick Warne and Company, but not before rewriting her stories in his own dreadful rhyming verse and giving them a rather moralising, sermonising tone. The vicar had already published a book of uplifting poetry for children: *Moral Rhymes for the Young*. However, the publishers weren't keen on his treatment either. In the end, Beatrix Potter decided to self-publish. In 1901 she had 250 copies printed of *The Tale of Peter Rabbit and Mr McGregor's Garden*.

However, Frederick Warne and Company decided to take another look at Beatrix's original text and illustrations. This time, they decided they quite liked them. Even so, they wanted the illustrations to be fewer in number and to be in colour rather than the original black and white. At first Beatrix resisted before finally going along with many, though not all of the publisher's suggestions.

Meanwhile her own 250 self-published copies had sold out, which no doubt further reassured Warne about the sales potential of the 'bunny book', as they called it. And so it was that after further discussion and negotiation *The Tale of Peter Rabbit* first appeared as a commercial publication in 1902. It was an immediate success. Beatrix was convinced that the book's triumph was in part due to the fact she had originally written it for a real little boy, Noel Moore, the son of her former governess, in 1893. The lesson learned, Beatrix would often trial a new story with the children of one her friends or relations.

More books appeared in quick succession. In 1903 two further tales were published: *The Tale of Squirrel Nutkin*, the first one of her books explicitly set in the Lake District, and *The Tailor of Gloucester*; 1904 saw the appearance of *The Tale of Benjamin Bunny* and *The Tale of Two Bad Mice*. Each new project found her working closely with her editor, Norman Warne, albeit much of it by letter. Even so, they managed to fall in love and become engaged, much to the dismay of her snobbish parents. Beatrix was now aged thirty-nine. And then tragedy. Again, uncannily mimicking Harriet Martineau's life story, barely a few weeks after Norman's marriage proposal, he died. Lymphatic leukaemia was the fatal diagnosis.

In total, Beatrix Potter wrote twenty-four Tales. Her sales then, as now, were huge. Her bestselling book, *The Tale of Peter Rabbit*, has sold over 40 million copies since it was first published in 1901. Being an astute business woman as well as a creative writer, Potter was canny enough to market and franchise her characters and a whole range of merchandise associated with them – dolls, colouring books, pottery, tea sets, wallpapers, board games. She patented Peter Rabbit as early as 1903, only a year after the commercial publication of the book in which he first appeared. But in 1936, when Walt Disney offered to adapt *The Tale of Peter Rabbit*, Potter said no. The idea of her creatures becoming cartoonish and no longer anatomically accurate was unthinkable.

However, towards the end of this twenty-odd year success story, she had had enough of rabbits and ducks, squirrels and mice. But her feelings for the Lake District hadn't diminished. If anything, her passion for the area had increased. She felt the pull of her ancestral roots ever stronger. Her biographer, Linda Lear, mentions a letter Potter wrote to an American friend in which she says 'I am descended from generations of Lancashire yeoman and weavers; obstinate, hard headed, *matter of fact* folk ...'

After their intended marriage, Beatrix and Norman planned to buy a small farm in the Lakes. Still in the early stages of grief, Potter nevertheless went ahead with the idea. She was keen to break free, at least in part, of some of the dull duties expected of a single Edwardian daughter.

With the help of her mounting book royalties, in 1905 she bought Hill Top Farm, an extended seventeenth-century cottage and its thirty-four acres. It lies on the edge of the little village of Near Sawrey between Windermere and the southern end of Esthwaite Water. The beauty, the slow tick of the rural clock, the richness of so much natural life held a deep appeal to Potter. Nevertheless, for much of the year she felt duty-bound to carry on living with her parents in London, able to write but unable to make the complete escape she longed for. But in spite of parental ties and family misgivings, she determined to become a fell farmer.

John Cannon, who had been running the farm on behalf of the previous owner, agreed to stay on and manage Hill Top while Potter set about learning how to raise sheep, cows, pigs and chickens. With advice from the Hawkshead solicitor William Heelis she went on to buy the adjacent Castle Farm and its cottage in 1909. Her regular dealings with Heelis brought them close. This new working and close relationship culminated in another proposal of marriage. Potter accepted William's offer and the couple wed on 15 October 1913 at the church of St Mary Abbots in Kensington, London. Beatrix formally became Mrs Potter Heelis. She was aged forty-seven; William forty-two.

Marriage finally allowed Potter to live full time in the Lake District. The couple moved into Castle Cottage, part of Castle Farm. However, Potter would still use the private quarters of Hill Top Farm to write and draw. Finally settled, Potter could immerse herself fully in country life, including wearing skirts and jackets made from the rough, rather scratchy wool of the Herdwick sheep – that sturdy, tough, agile ovine whose characteristics are so suited to living on the high fells and whose Cumbrian toughness so appealed to Potter. And instead of shoes she wore clogs. Her rustic look was complete.

Potter bought more land and pasture in the nearby Troutbeck valley on the other side of Windermere. She appointed the wise and respected Tom Storey to be her manager. Over the years she absorbed much of Tom's expertise in raising Herdwick sheep. In recognition of her growing knowledge and dedication, in 1942 she was elected president of the Herdwick Sheep Breeders' Association, founded in 1899 (as the Herdwick Sheep Association) by none other than Canon Hardwicke Rawnsley.

Although Canon Rawnsley might not have been much good as a children's poet, he remained friends with Potter until he died. Rawnsley was keen on preserving the traditional character of the Lakes. His opposition to the building of a railway line that would run through Borrowdale connecting the Honister slate quarries to the line at Braithwaite evolved into the Lake District Defence Society. The purpose of the society was to stop all 'injurious encroachments upon the scenery ... from purely commercial or speculative motives'. The preservationists and conservationists have always felt a sense of threat from the outside world. They worried that the more coarse and ugly sides of industry and progress would destroy what they saw as natural, pristine and timeless.

Later on in his life, Rawnsley became instrumental in helping to found the National Trust for Places of Historic Interest or Natural Beauty. He became the trust's first secretary. Influenced in part by Rawnsley's zeal for all things Cumbrian, Potter was also a keen supporter of preserving the character and traditions of the Lake District. And like Ruskin a generation before her, she gazed back in time and was keen to preserve the county's many traditional crafts and skills, not just the rearing of Herdwick sheep, but also the skills of furniture making, stoneworking and land management. As the years went by, Potter and her husband bought yet more farms, many sited at the heads of dales and valleys. By now she and her managers were farming thousands of sheep as well as Galloway cattle which, like the Herdwicks, were famed for their hardiness and their ability to live off the poorest of land.

Potter continued writing but her energies and interests continued to shift towards farming, conservation and Lake District life. She retained that shrewd, rational-thinking, scientific side of her character. She kept up-to-date with the latest veterinary ideas and tried new sheep dips. She was one of the first in the area to inject her sheep against the 'drop' or 'sheep staggers'. Indeed, she was quite happy to describe herself as a scientific farmer – anything to keep her beloved Herdwicks alive and well.

Potter remained a determined, blunt, often obstinate woman, characteristics that no doubt had helped her survive a lonely childhood and succeed, often against the odds, in becoming a successful writer and farmer of sheep. Potter's wonderful biographer, Linda Lear, wrote that:

She had a pragmatic understanding of the seasonable variability of climate and a deep appreciation of the fragile fell farm environment, but she also retained a romantic love of both inclement weather and the rugged landscape. She had a quiet acceptance that things will quite often go wrong, yet she had a remarkable patience and optimism. Loving the natural world as she did, Beatrix had long ago accepted that nature was wild, cruel and endlessly beautiful.

After thirty years of happy marriage and companionship, Beatrix Potter died of heart disease and pneumonia at Castle Cottage on 22 December 1943. She was aged seventy-seven. Eighteen months later, William Heelis also took ill and died on 4 August 1945. On their deaths, Beatrix and William left their sixteen farms, many cottages, over 4,000 acres, thousands of Herdwick sheep, and hundreds of Galloway cattle to the National Trust.

Chapter 20

A NATIONAL PROPERTY

Beatrix and William were just two – admittedly an influential and well-resourced two – in a long line of people who were anxious to preserve and conserve the beauty, culture and traditions of the Lake District. In his *Guide to the Lakes*, Wordsworth had written that he wanted the area to become 'a sort of national property, in which every man has a right and interest who has an eye to perceive and a heart to enjoy'. It would be this hope that echoed down the years.

Throughout the early decades of the twentieth century, there was growing interest in recognising certain parts of the country as wild, beautiful, worth visiting and good for people's wellbeing. There was resistance to any plan to turn beautiful and outstanding landscapes into factory-strewn eyesores or pine-forested wastelands. The Lake District in particular seemed in danger of being turned into one vast, dull, dark, impenetrable forest of conifers.

In 1931, Christopher Addison chaired a government committee that proposed a 'National Park Authority'. Its brief was to identify areas that might become national parks. Several aims were bound up with the idea. Protecting the landscape, its flowers and animals was certainly one of them. But there was also the wish to make the parks accessible to visitors. However, the general election of 1931 meant that the work of the committee was simply put on file.

It would take the end of the Second World War and the grow-ing mood for change to give a fresh boost to plans to open up the countryside for the benefit of everyone. The post-war Labour government was in favour of establishing national parks as part of its plans to reward a war-weary people and promote their welfare. The voluntary Standing Committee on National Parks had first met in 1936. There was opposition, of course. For example, in the Lake District, the Herdwick Sheep Breeders' Association wrote in 1939 opposing the idea.

It was a 1945 report by John Dower, the committee's secretary, that injected a head of steam into the plan to really have a go at creating national parks. He defined them as 'an extensive area of beautiful and relatively wild country' in which that beauty might be preserved, access for the public granted, wildlife and sympathetic buildings protected, and traditional farming maintained. In short, they had to be of 'high landscape quality'.

Two years later, the government set up its own committee chaired by Sir Arthur Hobhouse. It helped prepare legislation for the creation of a series of national parks. Twelve were proposed. They should be places of natural beauty, open to the public for leisure and recreation, and be accessible to city dwellers and those who wished to enjoy the peace and tranquillity of unspoilt countryside. Another two years later the National Parks and Access to the Countryside Act 1949 was passed with all-party support.

The Peak District National Park was the first to be established on 17 April 1951. Given the history of the Peaks and the pioneering actions of the ramblers who organised a mass trespass of Kinder Scout on 24 April 1932, in protest against wealthy landowners who were denying walkers and recreationalists access to the open countryside, it was fitting that the southern Pennines should become the first national park. The Peak ramblers would sing such tunes as 'The Trespassers Song' as they walked over hill and dale. It was actually written by the founder of the Sheffield

Clarion Ramblers, George Ward, and included the lines:

> There is no keeper in the Peak whom I could not lose.
> And if he watch'd me for a week, I'd tread the moor I choose.

Only three weeks later, on 9 May 1951, the second park, the Lake District National Park, was created. There are currently fifteen national parks. The Cairngorms is the largest in area, followed by the Lake District, which covers 912 square miles (2,362 square kilometres) of lakes and fells.

In July 2017, the Lake District became a UNESCO World Heritage Site. This puts it on a par with the Grand Canyon and the Great Barrier Reef, the Taj Mahal and Machu Picchu.

A partnership between the National Trust, the RSPB, the Lake District National Park Authority, and Cumbria Wildlife Trust submitted a petition for the Lake District to be granted world heritage status. The National Trust saw the Lakes as a unique landscape, one 'that has been shaped for centuries by people's activities – farming on the uplands and in the valley bottoms, quarrying and mining, forestry and water management, and tourism too. The result is a worked and continually changing landscape, or as we like to think an evolving masterpiece.' A few ecologists publicly opposed the idea on the grounds that it was favouring sheep over wildlife. Nevertheless, the bid was successful and there was much rejoicing by the members of the partnership. A 'national treasure' had received international recognition.

But not everyone was thrilled. There are environmentalists and ecologists who see too much of our landscape, including the Lake District, as overly managed. To be truly wild, nature must be allowed to take its own course. 'Rewilding' cannot take place, they argue, when men and women cut down woodland, plant regimented forests of fir and graze sheep.

One of the first to attack the decision was George Monbiot, a journalist, environmentalist, and political activist. He feared that the Lake District would be turned into 'a Beatrix Potter-themed sheep museum'. He went on to argue that, 'The entire high fells have been reduced by sheep to a treeless waste of cropped turf whose monotony is relieved only by erosion gullies, exposed soil and bare rock. Almost all the bird, mammal and insect species you might expect to find in a national park are suppressed or absent.' He went on. 'Sheep-worship' is only possible because of the massive support hill farmers receive from public monies. The romanticised picture of sheep and nature living in perfect harmony is plain wrong. 'Sheep, by nibbling out tree seedlings and other edible species, are a fully automated system for ecological destruction. They cleanse the land of almost all wildlife.'

Monbiot's protests follow in the tradition of some famous nature poets. In the mid-nineteenth century, John Clare wrote of his love for 'the commons left free in the rude rags of nature'. And a few decades later, in the 1880s, Gerard Manley Hopkins wrote:

What would the world be, once bereft
Of wet and of wildness? Let them be left,
O let them be left, wildness and wet;
Long live the weeds and wilderness yet.

At the end of the last Ice Age, around 7,000 to 8,000 years ago, the Lake District was covered by trees, carpeting the valleys and cloaking the hills up to a height of roughly 2,000 feet (600 metres). The higher fells were places where juniper bushes, dwarf willows and grasses grew among the rocks and stones. But then men and women arrived on the scene and things began to change.

The physical geographers Roy Millward and Adrian Robinson wrote that throughout the ages, from Neolithic times to the present, men and women have brought about fundamental changes in the vegetation and appearance of the Lake District by their 'destruction of the former woodlands. ... Much of the present poor grassland of the upland fells, for example, is the end-product of thousands of years of pastoral mismanagement'. By cutting down so much woodland and forest, Bronze Age farmers changed the character of the very soils themselves as the hummus-rich brown earths of the forest floor gave way to pale leached soils so characteristic of the uplands today.

In an equally powerful polemic, Mark Cocker notes our love of wildlife even as we witness its frightening decline. Of the 3,816 British species studied in the report 'State of Nature' (which pooled data and expertise from more than fifty nature conservation and research organisations), 60 per cent have declined over the past fifty years, much of the blame being placed at the door of industrial agri-businesses and moneyed landowners. Perhaps the saddest statistic is the almost complete loss of our wildflower meadows and the colour and joy they once brought to poets, painters, flittering butterflies, frolicking children and dewy-eyed lovers.

Twenty thousand years ago the 'natural' look of the Lake District was a vast ice sheet with not a tree in sight. Seven thousand years ago it was a place of continuous woodland up to a height of a couple of thousand feet. Today, its wild, craggy beauty is the result of thousands of years of tree felling and sheep grazing. This is a reminder that all landscapes are dynamic, fashioned by nature and shaped by man.

A couple of weeks after reading Monbiot, I came across James Rebanks' 2015 bestseller, *The Shepherd's Life: A Tale of the Lake District*. Rebanks lives in Matterdale. He farms Herdwick sheep, on the fells, helped by his dogs. He gets about on a quad bike. He's on UNESCO's panel for sustainable tourism. Not surprisingly, Rebanks sees things rather differently to Monbiot.

Rebanks' family have farmed in the Lake District for 600 years or more. The complex skills involved when farming mountain sheep have been passed down from father to son over the generations. The book is a lovely read. We follow the life of a shepherd through the four seasons, and along the way Rebanks tells his own story as he grows from boy to man.

However, as he begins his tale, the reader — well at least this one — is left feeling a little uncomfortable, chastened even, as James has gentle digs at those of us who romanticise the mountains and lakes, the rivers and skies. No one, says the shepherd, who works high on the fells or through winter storms 'romanticises wilderness'.

Rebanks reminds us that, above all, the Lake District is 'a peopled landscape', one shaped by men and women as they work the dales and fells and make their living. The poet and writer Norman Nicholson, born in Millom and who died in 1987 at the age of seventy-three, had a similar, albeit mystical, belief that the life of Cumbria's men and women was inextricably bound with their landscape: 'out of the rocks comes the true Lakeland life'. In contrast, most tourists are fair-weather folk, who disappear when the rains lash and the winds howl, the snow drifts and the ice freezes. But Rebanks thinks that the farmers' and shepherds' sense of belonging relates to how much weather they have endured: 'we belong here because the wind, rain, hail, snow, mud and storms couldn't shift us'.

At school, he was shocked to learn that the outside world saw the Lakes only through the eyes of the romantic poets, the tourist guides, privileged travellers and rich incomers. The farmers, the shepherds, the 'natives', seemed not to be part of the story. Wainwright, he comments, barely mentions or draws the things that farmers care about. For him, thought Rebanks, the Lake District was a place of escape. For others, it was a place to 'have adventures in other people's landscapes'.

Rebanks wanted to reclaim the landscape and its history for the modest, hard-working 'nobodies' who had lived among the hills for centuries, going back to the Vikings, to the ancient Britons. He wanted to give the farmers and shepherds their own voice, to explain and share their world. He grew up thinking that that the locals don't control their own story. And if you can't control your own story, then somebody else will, often not in a way that serves your interests or works to your advantage. So first he tweeted about his life and work, then he wrote *The Shepherd's Life*.

He reminds the tourists, the walkers, the romantics, that it was farmers who built the dry-stone walls, cleared the trees and drained the land to create the patchwork of meadows down in the dales where hay can be grown and sheep fed in winter and fattened for sale. 'Landscapes like ours,' he writes, 'are the sum total and culmination of a million little unseen jobs.' Remember that, we are told, when we wander o'er hill and dale.

Those who work in the countryside don't see the hills and fields as landscape. 'The very idea of landscape,' says the cultural theorist Raymond Williams, 'implies separation and observation.' Rebanks admonishes us. We have to see, understand and respect the indigenous culture and the way of life that the landscape signifies. 'What you don't see, you don't care about.' When you peer down from on high, think about the people and the landscape they have helped create. Listen to their story. So he tells it.

Clearly there is a tension between these two views: Monbiot the rewilder; Rebanks the working shepherd. As a lover of the Lake District I'm caught in the middle. I'd not really thought much about how even the higher fells were man-made and sheep-shaped. They simply look beautiful. But there I go, romanticising this ancient landscape, forgetting that it is home and the place of work for the shepherd and his family. The Lake District is a place where big themes are often played out – the wild and raw, the civilised and tamed. It is a hybrid landscape, neither wholly natural nor entirely manufactured. It still manages to combine extraordinary beauty even as it has been fashioned by farmers over the millennia.

These themes are beautifully explored by Sarah Hall in her 2015 novel *The Wolf Border,* in which zoologist Rachel Caine becomes involved with the reintroduction of wolves to Cumbria. Although apex predators like the wolf may be good for biodiversity and a healthy environment, they pose a challenge to farmers and their practices. Rachel sees England's countryside as little more than a series of gardens for its cities. Instead: 'She would like to believe there will be a place, again, where the streetlights end and wildness begins. The wolf border.'

Greater forces still will probably determine the long-term fate of this ever-evolving world. The country's economic fortunes wax and wane. Climate change will affect the temperature, the rainfall, the growth of the grass, the waters that run-off of the hills, the flooding of the rivers and the valleys. Ideologies come and go. Change happens but traditions hold things in place. Preservation of the man-made past doesn't square easily with the return of the wild.

Chapter 21

TALES AND SAILS

Hills, lakes and woods; hidden places and wild open spaces; remote farms and hardy sheep; magical worlds and the prospects of adventure. It is perhaps no surprise that the Lake District seems to have inspired not just poets and philosophers, arts and crafts, but also writers of children's stories.

Although in his time Robert Southey was best known as one of the Lake poets, he is perhaps better remembered today as the author of *The Story of the Three Bears*. It was first published as a stand-alone tale in 1837. Variations of the story had been around throughout much of the early nineteenth century. Southey's rendition was gentler in tone than some earlier, more frightening versions. In many of the original stories it was an old woman who entered the bear's house. But eventually she was replaced by the young and pretty Goldilocks, while the original three male bachelor bears evolved into a Mummy, Daddy and Baby Bear. Altogether more cosy and proper.

Harriet Martineau also had a go at writing children's books. Along with her essays, books on sociology, major works on economics, translations, countless newspaper articles, her guide to the Lake District and any number of pamphlets, she also found time to write a few children's stories. Most were written while she was in Tynemouth and feeling unwell. Titles included *The Billow and the Rock*, *The Settlers at Home*, *The Prince and the Peasant*, *Feats on the Fjord* and *The Crofton Boys*. The books are collectively known as The Playfellow series. However, when she had recovered and started her new life in Ambleside, she put away childish things, albeit with some reluctance, or so she seems to say in the preface to her 1853 reissue of *Settlers at Home*:

> The PLAYFELLOW was written, twelve years ago, to relieve the sense of uselessness; and the employment was so far agreeable to me, that I half promised to carry on the series if I should ever regain strength enough for the purpose. The strength was regained long ago; but health has brought new business and more imperative duties than chatting with little children, – alluring and not altogether useless as that amusement is. ... My first readers are grown up out of knowledge. If I am to be blessed with another series of juvenile friendships through these volumes, I shall feel them to be among the most fortunate of my writings; for there are few things in life better than a cordial understanding between author and readers; and the more unsophisticated the readers, the more precious is the author's privilege.

> Ambleside, July 1853

Politically, Robert Southey and Harriet Martineau were opposites. As he grew older, Southey's views became more conformist. In contrast, the more strident Martineau remained committed to equality, social change and the rights of women. She saw herself more as a scientific rationalist than a poetical romantic. Being Martineau, she couldn't resist introducing social messages and moral lessons into her children's stories. And to some extent this is true for Beatrix Potter too, although in Potter's case, the underlying political tone is one that values tradition and conservation. She found the militant suffragettes alarming and the thought of radical social change appalling. There are also more than enough hints that she recognised that nature really is red in both tooth and claw. The violence in her stories, though, comes twee-coated.

Beatrix Potter's very first story, *The Tale of Peter Rabbit*, is quite clear about what a dangerous place the world is if you are a rabbit. Other creatures want to eat you.

Peter's mother is a widow. His father was killed by Mr McGregor, the gardener, who caught the buck and baked him in a pie. Peter's mother warns her three daughters and Peter never to go into Mr McGregor's garden. But Peter is tempted by the vegetables and disobeys. Mr McGregor spots him and tries to catch the young rabbit. Peter is terrified. He has a number of narrow escapes, loses his clothes, sneaks past a lurking cat, before finally finding safety by wriggling under the gate. When he finally gets home, he feels sick. His mother is not impressed. His obedient sisters are rewarded with a splendid dinner of milk and berries. Peter is given only a cup of medicinal chamomile tea.

This raw element in Potter's writing was not lost on her readers. In his 1971 autobiography, *A Sort of Life*, Graham Greene recalls reading her tales as a boy:

> At an earlier period of course there was Beatrix Potter. I have never lost my admiration for her books and I have often reread her, so that I am not surprised when I find in one of my own stories, *Under The Garden*, a pale echo of Tom Kitten being trounced up by the rats behind the skirting-board and the sinister Anna-Maria covering him with dough, and in *Brighton Rock* the dishonest lawyer, Prewitt, hungrily echoes Miss Potter's dialogue as he watches the secretaries go by carrying their little typewriters.

Other writers have also appreciated Potter's use of language. When asked what books had the greatest influence on her writing, the novelist Penelope Lively answered in a *Guardian* article: 'Many. But I have to cite the Beatrix Potter titles, which showed me the arresting use of language.' And perhaps a little shyly, in another *Guardian* piece which asked past winners of the Man Booker Prize to recall their feelings at the time of their success, Margaret Atwood says, 'I probably shouldn't have said that my earliest literary influence was Beatrix Potter – however true – but I wasn't expecting to win. I had no [acceptance] speech prepared.'

The rabbits in the illustrated stories are exquisitely drawn by Potter. She was a talented scientific illustrator who early on in her career had become particularly skilled at drawing plants, fossils and particularly fungi. Her drawings of mushrooms and toadstools are beautifully executed both in colour and detail.

In her own work, Potter always saw science and art going hand in hand. She drew her animals – Peter Rabbit, Squirrel Nutkin, and Jemima Puddle-duck – naturalistically, albeit they wore frocks, bonnets and jackets. And again, in terms of their natures, Potter cleverly mixes their animal instincts with human emotions. Her biographer Linda Lear writes that Potter 'had in fact created a new form of animal fable: one in which anthropomorphic animals behave as real animals with true animal instincts ... her portrayal speaks to some universal understanding of rabbity behaviour.'

There is definitely a no-nonsense, get-on-with-it quality to Beatrix Potter. Her success coupled with her less than warm and loving childhood meant that she valued independence. She believed in the importance of good breeding, both for her animals and her fellow human beings if they were to produce good, healthy stock. She was intolerant of 'the lower orders' who turned to drink. She disliked shirkers. They are the 'undeserving' poor.

Settled on her farm, beneath the hills, Potter had become a wholesome countrywoman who championed country ways. All those who set about life with equal vim and vigour got her support. Girl Guides were allowed to camp in her fields. Factory workers who walked the fells got her support, so long as there were not too many of them and they closed the gates behind them.

* * *

Arthur Ransome's fictional children – John, Susan, Titty and Roger – certainly have vim and vigour. They are an adventurous crew. Their feral lives seem to reflect Arthur's own spirited approach to life, which he captures in all his children's stories, including, and especially *Swallows and Amazons* (1930).

Arthur was born on 18 January 1884 in Leeds, the eldest of four children. His father was a professor of history at the Yorkshire College of Science which eventually merged with the Leeds School of Medicine in 1884, the year of Arthur's birth. After various associations with other colleges in Manchester and Liverpool, the Yorkshire College was granted its own charter as an independent institution and in 1904 became the newly founded University of Leeds.

Many of the family's holidays were taken in the Lake District. When he was old enough, Arthur was sent to school in Windermere before he moved on to Rugby, albeit long after the days of the charismatic headmaster Thomas Arnold, late of Fox How, Ambleside. Arthur's father died prematurely when his son was just thirteen years old. Nevertheless, a few years later Arthur took himself off to study at Yorkshire College where his father had taught. But his time there wasn't a success and Arthur left after only a year.

He went off to London and took on various low-paying jobs working in the publishing industry. Although his career in publishing lasted only eighteen months the experience gave him the confidence to begin writing his own magazine articles and books. His initial efforts ranged across biographies, literary criticism and books for children. He married Ivy Constance Walker in 1909. They had a daughter, Tabitha, but divorced in 1924.

Arthur was involved in a prolonged court battle throughout 1913. Lord Alfred Douglas brought a libel case against Ransome for his biography of Oscar Wilde. Although Arthur eventually won the case, the experience was stressful. By way of a complete change, as 1913 was coming to a close Arthur went off to Russia to study Russian folklore. In 1916 he published *Old Peter's Russian Tales*.

The First World War broke out in 1914. Arthur turned journalist and became a foreign correspondent for *The Daily News*, the same radical, left-leaning paper for which Harriet Martineau had written her 1,640 feature articles. Arthur headed for the Eastern Front and by 1917 he found himself reporting on the Russian Revolution where he met many of its leaders, including Vladimir Lenin and Leon Trotsky. He also had dealings with Trotsky's personal secretary, Evgenia Petrovna Shelepina. It was Evgenia whom he would next marry.

Arthur's life became even more thrilling in the years after the First World War. To all intents and purposes he became a spy. His good relationships with the Russian Bolsheviks meant that he came in possession of all kinds of information that was of interest to MI5. In their files they gave him the code name S.76. However, the secret services were never entirely sure where Arthur's political sympathies lay and they kept a wary eye and open file on him. Arthur even looked the part. He had a walrus moustache, smoked a pipe and had a roving spirit. For a while he lived in Estonia with Evgenia.

It was while he was living in the Baltic that he had his first yacht built, which he named *Racundra*. His experiences sailing the yacht resulted in a book, *Racundra's First Cruise*, which was published in 1923 with some success.

Now remarried and looking for a quieter life, in 1924 he returned to England and took a job as a journalist with the *Manchester Guardian*. He bought an old beamed cottage at Low Ludderburn, a mile or so inland to the east of Windermere. This was where, in 1929, he began to write his most famous books, the Swallows and Amazons series. Although the first five books were set in the Lake District, Ransome's move to Suffolk in 1935 saw some of the later sailing adventures taking place on the Norfolk Broads, the North Sea, South China and the Hebrides.

The first book in the series, actually titled *Swallows and Amazons*, introduces the children of two holidaying families – the Walkers and the two Blackett sisters. There are lots of adventures in which the children sail, camp, fish, make up imaginative games, explore, play at being pirates, and generally have a jolly and exciting time. Dastardly things do happen but the children sort them out. All in all, the children have great fun living a wild, feral life until their holidays are over.

At the outbreak of the Second World War, Arthur and Evgenia first moved back to the Lake District, then over the next few years took properties in London and Cumbria, before finally buying Hill Top Cottage near Ealinghearth in the Rusland Valley, just a couple of miles west of the very southern tip of Windermere. Buying houses named Hill Top seems the thing to do if you are a writer of children's stories.

Arthur continued to write stories and books about fishing until his health began to fail. He died on 3 June 1967, aged eighty-three. He is buried with Evgenia, who died eight years later, in St Paul's churchyard in the village of Rusland, not far from Hill Top Cottage. His books, like those of Beatrix Potter, became bestsellers. He received many awards and honours, including a CBE and honorary doctorate from the University of Leeds – a nice touch given that his father had taught there when it was the Yorkshire College, and Arthur himself had spent a less than glorious year there as an undergraduate.

* * *

In a curious, but rather delightful book, *Another Country* (2008), James Mackenzie has mapped both the geographical and literary landscapes of the Lake District. He writes about all the children's books, or at least as many as he can find, that have been set in Cumbria. By 2008, he had found 155 stories in which children have holidays, fun and adventures on the lakes, by the rivers and over the hills. He finds out in which part of the Lakes each story takes place and then takes the reader on a brief topographical tour of that location, hence his subtitle: *A Guide to the Children's Books of the Lake District and Cumbria.*

There are too many authors to name them all. We have already met the more obvious candidates, including Beatrix Potter and Arthur Ransome. But how about Angela Brazil, Rosemary Sutcliff, Elsie J. Oxenham, John Rowe Townsend, Lorna Hill and Elfrida Vipont? And over at Fox How, the holiday home of the talented Arnold family, Thomas Arnold's granddaughter Mary began writing under her married name, Mrs Humphrey Ward. She became a novelist. Poetry and prose seemed to run in her family. Her sister's son was Aldous Huxley.

In 1881 Mary published a book for children set in the Lake District; *Milly and Olly; or, A Holiday Among the Mountains.* She describes Fox How as a 'modest' house of ten bedrooms and three sitting rooms with a magnificent view of the Fairfield Horseshoe, although I'm not sure how easy it would be to see the mountains today, the house surrounded as it is by a wood of mature trees. In her story, Fox How is fictionalised as Ravensnest. I can't resist quoting a few sentences from the book as they give a sense of the life of upper-class Victorian children:

> "Milly, come down! Come down directly! Mother wants you. Do make haste!"

"I'm just coming Olly. Don't stamp so. Nurse is tying my sash."

Their mother, Mrs Norton, tells them they're about to go off on holiday. The children want to go to the seaside, but their mother has other ideas:

> "No, we're not going to the sea this summer. We are going to a place mother loves better than the sea, though perhaps you children mayn't like it quite so well. We're going to the mountains …
>
> these are English mountains, kind easy mountains, not too high for you and me to climb up, and covered all over in soft green grass and wild flowers, and tiny sheep with black faces."

Now doesn't that sound lovely, Herdwick sheep and all?

Similarly, James Mackenzie introduces his review with an enticing quote from Geoffrey Trease's book, *The Gates of Bannerdale*, based on Wasdale and first published in 1956. In the story, Penny and Bill return home to the Lake District each holiday to be welcomed by the familiar panorama:

> The train rattled on, the sea came into view on our left and the well-remembered shapes of the mountains on our right. The spring was later here, but there were daffodils already under the apple trees. The fells, crouched like great friendly dogs, still wore their last autumn coats of shaggy brown bracken, but very soon now the new green stalks would be pushing up and unfolding.

Again, who could resist? Like the writers he discovers, James Mackenzie believes the Lake District to be 'a magical setting for children's stories' and so he is not surprised to find the meres and mountains exciting the imagination and conjuring so many adventures. Of the 113 books published by Geoffrey Trease, five were set in and around Wastwater.

Marjorie Lloyd's Lakeland books roam in and around the rivers and hills of Skelwith Bridge on the River Brathay, beneath the beautiful cascading waterfalls of Skelwith Force. They tell of the adventures of the five Browne children. Their parents are in India and the children are sent to holiday with Mr and Mrs Jenks on their farm, hence the Fell Farm series of books, all published in the early 1950s. Good outdoor types, the Browne children are always walking by rivers, playing over fells and hiking in their hobnailed boots.

And so on, story after story, by authors who have all been inspired by the drama of Lakeland. Even, albeit at a much gentler pace, *Postman Pat*, who lived in the idyllic, fictional village of Greendale. For several years, John Cunliffe lived in Kendal. His dozens and dozens of *Postman Pat* books, based on the original television series, are based on village life as he found it in the dales that ran down into Kendal, delighting generations of younger readers and their television viewing habits.

* * *

There is a walk I enjoy taking around the base of Loughrigg Fell. It's not exactly a literary walk, but in over just a few miles I pass by the houses and holiday homes of a surprising number of writers … and literary genres.

The walk begins in Ambleside not far from The Knoll, the home of Harriet Martineau. I cross Miller Bridge over the River Rothay and take the path up Loughrigg Fell by Todd Crag, before dropping down into Skelwith Bridge where Marjorie Lloyd wrote the Fell Farm books. The route from Skelwith Bridge takes me by Loughrigg Tarn and Scroggs Cottage, now Nook House, where Jonathan Otley was born and took his holidays. The walk then leads me along the shores of Grasmere and on to the village. From there I head back along the 'coffin route' to Ambleside, first passing Dove Cottage where William Wordsworth wrote many of his poems and Coleridge managed to pen a few of his, and where later the rental was picked up by Thomas De Quincey. A mile or so further on, the path drops down beside Rydal Mount, Wordsworth's final home. From there it's only twenty minutes before you return to Ambleside, passing The Knoll once more.

Just six miles and a wander through 200 years of poems, autobiographies, guidebooks, children's stories, polemical tracts, and so much literary talent.

Chapter 22

INTIMATIONS OF MORTALITY

Although it's cold and a film of fragile ice is beginning to crackle around the edges, Lily Tarn looks enchanted and serene. The air tingles with frost. There is no wind and the sky is a pale sapphire. The sun is slipping behind distant Wetherlam, adding a soft pink and orange glow to the thin winter blue. I'm sitting on a rock by the tarn. There is no one else about. I seem to have Loughrigg Fell to myself. I love this spot.

There is something missing though. As long as I can remember, a small silver birch, slender and slight, grew on the little island that sits in the middle of the tarn. Looking south across the water, the picture the tree helped compose was one of other-worldly beauty. And now it had fallen, presumably in one of the year's earlier winter storms. It lies toppled, its slim, sodden trunk and branches gradually being lost to the cold mountain waters.

It was a sad, poetic reminder not only of beauty faded but also of life's transience. Jonathan Otley's friend and physician, Dr David Lietch, in similar mood captures something of the passing of another beautiful life when he describes the old clock repairer's growing fragility. Otley was trying to take his annual measurement of the lake level of Derwent Water. Lietch watched as the eighty-six-year-old man suddenly slipped. As reported by Tom Smith in his biography of Jonathan Otley, Dr Lietch later recalled the scene:

The evening light, the low calm, almost silent waters of the lake – for they scarcely lapped against the crag at his feet – the rough track he was treading, and all the sights and sounds which in this valley accompany the close of the day, were in harmony with the idea of the old man. The waters of life were low with him now, weak as the ripple scarcely breaking the rock, yet they were calm and bright withal. ... The similitude between the hour and the man, the sunset and the departing life, became so impressive, that it was an unpleasant shock to see him slip and fall on the rock, as though life had so nearly toppled over the shores of time.

But as Wordsworth wrote in his ode 'Intimations of Immortality', as our days pass, life goes on and we must be grateful:

What though the radiance which was once so bright
Be now for ever taken from my sight,
Though nothing can bring back the hour
Of splendour in the grass, of glory in the flower;
We will grieve not, rather find
Strength in what remains behind;

Throughout these pages we have seen how the Lake District repeatedly inspires reflection and strong feelings – aesthetic, cultural, political, emotional, environmental, ecological, scientific. The drama of the landscape seems to stretch the imagination. Our emotions are pulled, our wonder heightened, our curiosity fired. We live for a moment in an infinitely expanded, vibrant present.

The philosopher Don Cupitt has explored how we shape as well as how we are shaped by the language we use, including the way we describe, experience and see all that there is around us. It is as we contemplate the outer landscape, our internal landscape of self and sense, thought and feeling, change. Deeper notes of understanding become possible. And as we understand more deeply and feel more profoundly, so our resonance and oneness with the world increases. This was how Wordsworth and Coleridge thought about poetry. Sublime landscapes of wonder can and do influence who we are. There is a reflexive relationship between contemplating nature's beauty and deepening our consciousness of self. Inner subjective experience and outer objective understanding meld; the world and our being in it become one. Thus, the living of life itself becomes the source of its own meaning. Those with an 'ecological consciousness' understand the interconnectedness of all things and that we separate ourselves from nature at our peril.

On wild mountain peaks, beneath vast skies, on the edge of an endless ocean, we feel thrillingly small, ecstatically meaningless in the face of the world's beautiful, boundless disinterest in our brief existence. In such places, our fleeting lives, says Cupitt, feel both infinitely important and infinitely *un*important. In places of remote beauty and vast horizons, the boundary between the self and the world of land, lake and sky dissolves. The senses are overwhelmed by moments of pure ecstasy.

Another philosopher, Julian Baggini, also feels that:

> the most intense aesthetic experiences actually have their power precisely because they remind us of our mortality. Being overwhelmed in a powerful experience of the here and now makes the transitory nature of existence evident and thus brings home to us the fact that the very possibility of experience itself will come to an end.

Nan Shepherd knew all about such feelings. In her 1977 book *The Living Mountain* she writes about her time on and among the Cairngorms of Scotland. For her, walking is 'a journey into Being; for as I penetrate more deeply into the mountain's life, I penetrate also into my own. For an hour I am beyond desire ... I am not out of myself, but in myself: I am.' For Shepherd, 'place and mind may interpenetrate until the nature of both are altered'. The tarns and mountains of the Lake District have a similar power to bring about feelings of transcendence and a boundless sense of self. Subject and object become caught in an inflationary loop of sensory excitement in which the self feels both lost and infinite.

The soft evening light begins to leave Lily Tarn. The sun has set. I can see a mist beginning to form in the valleys below. It's all so exquisitely, tearfully beautiful. I laugh. But then it's time to go.

I climb up one of the craggy tops by the tarn for one last panoramic gaze. The mists are settling over Ambleside. I look across to Harriet Martineau's The Knoll, but it has already disappeared under the creeping fog. Beyond, on the banks of the River Rothay, Fox How too is now lost to the silence of the muffling white. The tops of the Fairfield Horseshoe are snow-capped and rose-tinted as they catch the last rays of the winter sun.

Somewhere in the mists beneath Heron Pike and Nab Scar is Rydal Mount, where William, Dorothy and Mary Wordsworth lived for so long before they left their own lives behind, but as I make my way down, all I can see below is the spire of Sir George Gilbert Scott's neo-Gothic church, St Mary's as it rises ghostly through the mist.

John Dalton and Jonathan Otley would have been fascinated by the fog as it slowly blankets the village and valley below. And although Wordsworth in his poem 'The Excursion' could write of 'vapours' under 'cerulean' skies, and of 'Clouds, mists, streams, watery rocks and emerald turf, / Clouds of all tincture, rocks and sapphire sky', Dalton's and Otley's thoughts were equally wonderful. Dalton never lost his fascination for clouds and vapours, mists and fogs. It was his interest in meteorology in general and clouds in particular that got him thinking about very small things and their behaviour, about atoms and their properties. Out of the cloudy skies and misty hills of the Lake District was born the science of atoms and the foundations of chemistry.

There is no right or proper way to contemplate nature. Poets and painters, sages and scientists all add insight and understanding to the world around us. Bryan Magee sees both the arts and sciences as 'truth-seeking activities ... penetrating beneath the surface of appearances.' Their success requires imagination, the ability, as Einstein said, not only to observe but 'to "feel" into things'. We can feel our spirits rise as we look up at the snow settling over Hay Stacks, or sit quietly on the shores of Ullswater on a windless day, or marvel at the crystals of feldspar as they sparkle in a sun-flamed granite at Shap or gaze across the fell tops to the distant sea.

The walk down the slopes of Loughrigg Fell is steep but quick. The mist is thick now. I don't see the stone parapet of Miller Bridge until I cross the slippery rails on the cattle-grid, a few metres before the path rises over the river. There is now a deep, creeping silence to the dense fog. By the time I walk through Rothay Park it has grown dark.

But there is a diffused light ahead. It brightens as I approach St Mary's, and as I pass through the churchyard I am surrounded by a white, opalescent glow. My jacket glistens with a million beads of dew. I stop. There is just the silence and a beautiful light.

BIBLIOGRAPHY

Atwood, Margaret (2018), 'How it feels to win the Man-Booker' *Guardian*, 30 June.

Baggini, Julian (2004), *What's It All About? Philosophy and the Meaning of Life*, London: Granta Books.

Barker, Juliet (2000), *Wordsworth: A Life*, London: Viking.

Bate, Jonathan (1991), *Romantic Ecology: Wordsworth and the Environmental Tradition*, London: Routledge.

Berlin, Isaiah (2013), *The Roots of Romanticism* (2nd edn), Princeton: Princeton University Press.

Boardman, John (1996), *Classic Landforms of the Lake District* (2nd edn), London: The Geographical Association.

Bragg, Melvyn (1983), *Land of the Lakes*, London: Secker and Warburg.

Cardwell, D. S. L. (ed.) (1968), *John Dalton and the Progress of Science*, Manchester: Manchester University Press.

Cocker, Mark (2018), *Our Place: Can We Save Britain's Wildlife Before It Is Too Late?*, London: Jonathan Cape.

Cupitt, Don (1997), *After God: The Future of Religion*, London: Weidenfeld and Nicolson.

Davies, Hunter (1999), *Beatrix Potter's Lakeland*, London: Warne.

Davies, Hunter (2009), *William Wordsworth* (rev. edn), London: Frances Lincoln.

Davies, Hunter (2016), *Lakeland: A Personal Journey*, London: Head of Zeus.

BIBLIOGRAPHY

Dennison, Matthew, (2016), *Over the Hills and Far Away: The Life of Beatrix Potter*, London: Head of Zeus.

Duveen, D. I. and Klickstein, H. S. (1955), John Dalton's Autobiography, *Journal of Chemical Education*, 32, p. 333.

Gannon, Paul (2009), *Rock Trails: Lakeland*, Caernarfon: Pesda Press.

Gilpin, William (1792), *Observations, Relative Chiefly to Picturesque Beauty, Made in the Year 1772 in several Parts of England, particularly the Mountains, and Lakes of Cumberland, and Westmoreland*, London: R. Blamire.

Gray, Thomas (1775), *Journal of a Visit to the Lake District in 1769.* In Toynbee, Paget and Whibley, Leonard et al. (eds), later additions by Starr, H. W. (1971), *Correspondence of Thomas Gray*, Oxford: Clarendon Press.

Greenaway, Frank (1966), *John Dalton and the Atom*, London: Heinemann.

Greene, Graham (1971), *A Sort of Life*, London: Bodley Head.

Hahn, Daniel (2009), *Poetic Lives: Coleridge*, London: Hesperus Press.

Hall, Sarah (2015), *The Wolf Border*, London: Faber and Faber.

Harrison, Melissa (2016), *Rain: Four Walks in English Weather*, London: Faber and Faber.

Hayhow, D. B. et al. (2016), 'State of Nature 2016', The State of Nature Partnership.

Henderson, Casper (2017), *A New Map of Wonders*, London: Granta.

Holmes, Richard (2008), *The Age of Wonder*, London: Harper Press.

Holmes, Richard (2016), *This Long Pursuit: Reflections of a Romantic Biographer*, London: William Collins.

Hopkins, G. M. (1881), 'Inversnaid' : In Bridges, R. (ed.) (1918) *Poems of Gerard Manley Hopkins*, London: Humphrey Milford.

Hunter, Shelagh, (1995), *Harriet Martineau: The Poetics of Moralism*, Aldershot: Scolar Press.

Lear, Linda (2006), *Beatrix Potter: The Extraordinary Life of a Victorian Genius*, London: Allen Lane.

Leslie, S. et al. (2015), 'The fine-scale genetic structure of the British population', *Nature* 519, pp. 309–14, 19 March (https://doi.org/10.1038/nature14230).

Lively, Penelope (2017), 'Books that made me', *Guardian*, 1 December.

Macfarlane, Robert (2007), *The Wild Places*, London: Granta Books.

Mackenzie, James (2008), *Another Country: A Guide to the Children's Books of the Lake District and Cumbria*, Coleford: Girls Gone By Publishers.

Magee, Bryan (2016), *Ultimate Questions*, Princeton: Princeton University Press.

Martineau, Harriet (1983/1887), *Harriet Martineau's Autobiography, Volume I*, London: Virago Press.

Millward, Roy, and Robinson, Adrian (1970), *The Lake District*, London: Eyre and Spottiswoode.

Monbiot, George (2014), *Feral: Rewilding the Land, Sea and Human Life*, London: Penguin.

Monbiot, George (2017), 'The Lake District's world heritage site status is a betrayal of the living world', *Guardian*, 11 July.

Nevill, John Cranstoun (1943), *Harriet Martineau*, London: Frederick Muller.

Olalde, Inigo et al. (2018), The Beaker phenomenon and the genomic transformation of northwest Europe, *Nature*, 21 February, doi:10.1038/nature25738.

Otley, Jonathan (1827), *A Concise Description of the English Lakes and Adjacent Mountains: with general directions to tourists* (3rd edn), London: John Richardson.

Pinker, Steven (2018), *Enlightenment Now: The Case for Reason, Science, Humanism, and Progress*, London: Allen Lane.

Radcliffe, Ann, and Bradshaw, Penny (ed.) (2015), *Observations During a Tour to the Lakes of Lancashire, Westmoreland, and Cumberland*, Carlisle: Bookcase.

Rebanks, James (2015), *The Shepherd's Life: A Tale of the Lake District*, London: Allen Lane.

BIBLIOGRAPHY

Reich, David (2018), *Who We Are and How We Got Here: Ancient DNA and the New Science of the Human Past*, Oxford: Oxford University Press.

Rollinson, William (1967), *A History of Man in the Lake District*, London: J. M. Dent and Sons.

Rovelli, Carlo (2016), *Reality is Not What it Seems: The Journey to Quantum Gravity*, London: Allen Lane.

Ruskin, John (1873), *Modern Painters, Volume 3*, London: John Wiley and Sons.

Smith, Thomas Fletcher (2007), *Jonathan Otley: Man of Lakeland*, Carlisle: Bookcase.

Thompson, Ian (2010), *The English Lakes: A History*, London: Bloomsbury.

Wainwright, Alfred (2003), *Memoirs of a Fellwanderer* (new edn), London: Francis Lincoln.

Webb, R. K. (1960), *Harriet Martineau: A Radical Victorian*, London: Heinemann.

West, Thomas (1778), *A Guide to the Lakes in Cumberland, Westmorland, and Lancashire*, London: Richardson and Urquhart.

Westwood, Robert (2009), *The Geology of the Lake District: An Introduction*, Alderholt: Inspiring Places Publishing.

Wheatley, Vera (1957), *The Life and Work of Harriet Martineau*, London: Secker and Warburg.

Wilson, Frances (2016), *Guilty Thing: A Life of Thomas De Quincey*, London: Bloomsbury.

Woodcock, Nigel, and Strachan, Rob (eds) (2012), *Geological History of Britain and Ireland* (2nd edn), London: Wiley-Blackwell.

ACKNOWLEDGEMENTS

Many thanks to Sara Hunt of Saraband for her interest and support. Sara's early encouragement, advice and savvy suggestions have been much appreciated. Also huge thanks to my editor, Charlotte Cole, for her keen eyes and helpful ideas on how and where the text could be reshaped, sharpened and improved. Thank you to Jei Degenhardt for proofreading. Steve Matthews, as well as running Bookcase publications, is also family co-owner of the wonderful Bookends bookshop in Carlisle. Its labyrinthine splendour is packed with thousands and thousands of books, including many specialising in subjects related to the Lake District. I owe Steve a big debt of gratitude for his initial interest and generosity over this venture.

Although I never had the chance to meet Barbara Todd, I did meet Maureen Colquhoun, who also lives at The Knoll, Harriet Martineau's old home. Maureen, economist and former MP, was kind enough to invite me into their house and show me the room, with its lovely view across the Rothay valley, where Martineau read and wrote so prolifically. It was a special moment. I paid several visits to the excellent Armitt Museum in Ambleside and Keswick Museum. Thanks to all those who help run and support these superb resources.

Thanks, too, to my children and their partners – Jacob and Angela, Rebecca and Matt – for their continued willingness to join me walking the fells and sharing my love of the Lakes. And finally, love and thanks to my granddaughters, Elsa and Lucy, the next generation of fell walkers, whose energy and enthusiasm is guaranteed to keep even these old bones going that one more mile.

D. H.

INDEX

Addingham 109
Addison, Christopher 178
African plate 86–87
Age of Enlightenment, the 8
Age of Sensibility, the 8
Agricola, Julius 104
Alfoxton House, Somerset 27
Allan Bank, Grasmere 40, 43, 171
Alps 86, 93, 117, 124
Altrincham 1
Ambleside 1, 4, 14, 105–106, 113, 120, 128, 131, 147, 150, 151, 153, 154, 187, 195–196, 200–201
ammonites 84
Angle Tarn 92
Anglia Ruskin University 165
Anglian ice sheet 89–90
Anglo-Saxons 108–112, 163
Arctic charr 61
Ardnamurchan 85
Ardwick cemetery 12
arêtes 92
Armbroth 3
Armbroth Fell 65
Arniston Crag 136
Arnold, Matthew 147, 152

Arnold, Dr Thomas 147, 190, 193
art 8
Arts and Crafts Movement 161, 164
Asra see Hutchinson, Sara
Atlantic Ocean 68
Atlas (Greek deity) 68
atomic theory of matter 9–13
atoms 10–13
Atwood, Margaret 189
Avalonia 67–72, 74, 78–79

Baddeley, M.J.B. 133, 135
Baggini, Julian 199
Baltica 67, 69, 79
Barker, Juliet 48, 50–51
Bassenthwaite Lake 53, 54, 60
Bate, Jonathan 49, 128, 164
Beaker people 100
Beardsall, Eric 137
Beddoes, Dr Thomas 28
Berlin, Isaiah 19
Big Chill Swim 54
Biggs, Stanton 51
birdlife 60
Birthwaite 118
Black Combe 102, 133
Black Crags 102

Blackburn 136, 138
Blea Water 92
Blencathra 92, 100, 108
blind philosopher of Kendal, the see also Gough, John 8
Bolton 4
Borrowdale 63, 93, 120, 125 see also Rosthwaite
Borrowdale Volcanics 64–78, 85–86, 98
Boudica, Queen 104
Bow Fell 63, 91, 94
Bowles, Caroline 48
Bradshaw, Penny 125
Bragg, Melvyn 159
Braithwaite 112, 175
Brampton Railway 117
Brantwood 163, 165
Brathay Hall 40
Brathay, River 105, 195
Brigantes, the 103–105
Brigham 109
Bristol 21, 27, 28
Bristol Pneumatic Institute 28
Brompton by Sawdon 34
Brontë, Charlotte 151, 155
Bronze Age 100–102, 182
Brougham Castle 124

INDEX

Brown, Dr John 120
Buckland, William 158
Budworth, Joseph 123–124, 133
Burl, Aubrey 102
Burnett, George 26
Buttermere 54, 93, 159

Caesar, Julius 104
Cairngorms 180, 200
Caldbeck Fells 75
Calderas 73
Caledonian Orogeny 79
Caledonide Mountains 79–80, 86
Cambridge, University of 21, 23, 25, 50, 65, 120
Campbell, Donald 55–58
Campbell, Sir Malcolm 55
Cannon, John 174
Carlisle 105, 113–115, 117–118, 170
Carlisle Castle 115
Carlisle, Earl of 117
Carlisle Priory 113
Carlyle, Thomas 47, 146
Carrock Fell 76
Cartmel Priory 113
Carvetii Celtic tribe 103
Castle Cottage 174–175, 177
Castlenook mine 77
Castlerigg Fell 72
Castlerigg stone circle 100, 125

Celts 100–103, 105, 107–111
chemistry 6, 9–11, 35, 201
Chorley 4
Clare, John 19–20, 181
Claudius, Emperor 104
climate change 89–90, 185
cloud, formation 9
coal measures, Carboniferous 83
Cocker, Mark 182
Cocker, River 108
Cockermouth 7, 21, 114
Cockermouth Castle 159
coffin routes 113–114, 196
Coleridge, Derwent 34
Coleridge, Hartley
Coleridge, Samuel Taylor 16–17, 18, 20–21, 26–47, 126, 127, 128, 145, 171, 196, 199
Coleridge, Sara née Fricker 27, 30, 32, 36, 38, 47
Collingwood, W. G. 75
Comb Crags 2
Comb Gill 2
Combrogi, the 108
Compounds, chemical 10–11
Compte, Augustus 152–153

Coniston 75, 113, 119, 163
Coniston Fells 115: Old Man of Coniston 58, 94, 123, 133, 137
Coniston Water 53, 55–58, 159
Constable, John 40, 156
continental drift 82, 85
Cookson, Reverend William 25
corries 91
Crewe 6
Crinkle Crags 62, 94
Crosthwaite 112
Crummock Water 53, 159
crustal plates 70, 72, 79, 81–86
Cumberland pencil industry 77
Cumbria Way 93
Cunliffe, John 195
Cupitt, Don 198–199
curiosity 8, 18, 41, 65, 158, 198
cwms 91
Cymri 108

daffodils 38–40, 48, 150
Daily News, The 151, 152, 191
Dale, Thomas 158
Dalton Lecture, The 12
Dalton Nuclear Institute 12

Dalton, John 6–13, 14, 22, 64–65, 131, 200–201
Dalton, Dr John 117
Danby, Francis 37
Darwin, Charles 145, 163
David I, King 114
Davy, Humphry 18, 28–29, 35, 36
Dawson, Dr James 171
de Quincey, Thomas 40–42, 59, 196
Defoe, Daniel 116
Dennison, Matthew 169
Derwent, River 22, 108
Derwent Water 53, 58, 59–60, 159, 197
Devensian ice sheet 90
Dickens, Charles 152
dinosaurs 84
DNA population studies 100–101, 107, 111–112
Doggerland 96
Donelly, Peter 111
Dove Cottage 16, 30–32, 36, 40–41, 196
Dove Crag 138
Dovedale 93
Dower, John 179
Dunmail, King 109
Dunmail Raise 15, 61–62, 109
Durham, University of 48

Eaglesfield 7
Ealinghearth 192

Eamont Bridge 99
Easedale 15
Easedale Tarn 62
ecological conscious-ness 164, 180
ecological sensibility 49
Eden, River 108
Eden Valley 105
Edinburgh Review 40
Edmund, King 109
Einstein, Albert 201
elements, chemical 10
Eliot, George 155
Elizabeth I, Queen 75, 115
Elterwater slates 74
Emerson, Ralph Waldo 47
Ennerdale Water 53
environmental consciousness 49–50
environmentalism 156, 166
Esk, River 104, 108
Eskdale 72, 105
Esthwaite Water 54, 174
Eurasian tectonic plate 82, 84
Ewanrigg 101

Fairfield 62, 133
Fairfield Horseshoe 45, 193, 200
Fell, Sheila 156
Fennimore, James 47
feudalism 114, 163
Fiennes, Celia 120
floods of 2015 15
Forncett, St Peter, Norfolk 25

Foster, Joseph 54
Fox How, Ambleside 52, 147, 152, 190, 193, 200
Foxie, the dog 36–38, 88
French Revolution 23
Fricker, Edith see Southey, Edith
Fricker, Sara, see Coleridge, Sara
Fry, Elizabeth 143, 155
Furness Abbey 114
Furness Railway Company 57

Galava, Roman fort of 52, 106
Garnett, John 131
genetic make-up of populations 100–101
geological history of Cumbria 63–87
geological maps and guides 64, 66, 131
German miners 75
Germany, tours of 30
Giant's Causeway 85
Giddens, Anthony 154
Gillman, James 46–47
Gilpin, William 123
Glannoventa 104
Glaramara 63, 67
glaciers and glaciation 53, 61, 89–94
Glenridding Beck 76
Glossop 170
Gondola (the yacht) 57–58
Gondwana 68

INDEX

Gough, Charles
36–37, 88
Gough, John 7–8, 131
Gowbarrow Park 38
granites 81
graphite 77
Grasmere 1, 4, 15, 26,
30, 52, 54, 60, 112,
113, 120–121, 196
Grasmere Common 62
gravity, water flow by
4–5
Gray, Effie 160–161,
165, 169
Gray, Thomas
120–121
Great Castle How 61
Great Gable 62, 63
Great Langdale 93, 98
green movement 166
Greene, Graham 188
Greenhow, Elizabeth
146
Greenhow, Thomas
146
greenstone 98–99
Greta Hall, Keswick
32, 34, 36, 38, 65
Greta, River 2, 75
Grisedale 112
Grisedale Tarn 54, 92
Grizedale 112
guides to the Lake
District 120–134

Hadrian, Emperor 105
Hadrian's Wall 107
Hagg Gill 106
Halifax 22, 25
Hall, Sarah 185
Hall, Spencer 146
Halliwell, Victor 55

Hamill, Captain Felix
58
Hardknott Pass
104–105
Hardknott Roman fort
104–106
Harrison, Melissa 15
Harter Fell 72
Hastings, Battle of 112
Haweswater 53,
106–107
Hawkshead Grammar
School 23
Hay Stacks 94,
141–142, 201
Heelis, William 174,
177, 178
Helm Crag 123
Helvellyn 1, 3, 4, 13,
36–37, 59, 62, 65,
76, 85, 89, 92–94,
123, 132
Henry II, King 114
Herdwick sheep 175,
176, 177, 179, 182,
194
Heron Pike 45, 52
Heyes Lane Primary
School, Timperley 39
High Rigg 94
High Seat 100
High Street 92, 94,
106
Hill Top Cottage 192
Hill Top Farm 174,
175
Hind Gill 63
Hobhouse, Sir Arthur
179
Hockney, David 141
Holmes, Richard 35
Honister slate 74, 175

Hopkins, Gerard
Manley 181
Howell, Sheila 58
Hunter, Shelagh 154
hunter-gatherers 97
Hutchinson, Mary see
Wordsworth, Mary
Hutchinson, Sara 32,
43–44, 47, 126

Iapetus Ocean 68–80
Iapetus suture 80, 85
Ice Age 53, 61, 81,
88–95, 181
ice ages, causes of 89
Iceni, the 104
industrial revolution
6, 11
Innominate Tarn 142
interglacials 89
Iron Age 102–103

Jackson, President
Andrew 145
James I, King 115
Jerrold, Douglas 149
Johnson, Linton Kwesi
154

Kant, Immanuel 8
Keats, John 18,
20–21, 46
Keble, Reverend John
48
Kendal 7–8, 26,
105–107, 118, 141,
195
Keswick 14, 15, 26,
38, 46, 49, 64–65,
75, 77, 109, 113,
114, 119, 120, 124,
128

Keswick Launch
  Company 58
Kirk Fell 72
Kirkhead Cave 96
Klee, Paul 159
Knapping, flint and
  tuff 97
'knock and lochan'
  terrain 92
Knoll, The, Ambleside
  143, 147, 151, 152,
  195, 196, 200, 206

Lady of the Lake,
  Ullswater 58–59
Lake District Defence
  Society 175
Lancaster 4
Lancaster and Carlisle
  Railway 118
land speed records 55
Landseer, Edward 37
Langdale Pikes 15,
  60–61, 63, 93, 98,
  133
Langstrath Beck 63
Latham, Dr Peter 153
laudanum 38, 43, 47
laughing gas 28–29
Laurentia 68–70,
  78–79, 84–85
Le Corbusier 164
Lear, Linda 174,
  176–177, 189
Leeds, University of
  190, 192
Lenin, Vladimir 191
Lietch, David 197–198
Lily Tarn 197, 200
Lingmoor Fell 92
Little Langdale 93,
  105, 115

Lively, Penelope 189
Lloyd, Marjorie 195,
  196
Lostock water
  treatment works 5
Loughrigg Fell 30, 92,
  147, 195, 197, 201
Loughrigg Tarn 64,
  196
Low Ludderburn 192
Lower Borrowdale
  Volcanic Group
  71–72, 94
Loweswater 54
Lowry, L. S. 156
Lowther, Sir James 22
Lyrical Ballads: volume
  I 28; volume II
  28–29

Macfarlane, Robert 20
Mackenzie, James
  193–195
Magee, Brian 201
Malcolm I, King 109
Malcolm III, King 113
Malcolm IV, King
Manchester 1, 2, 3–6,
  9–10, 12, 37, 41,
  117, 168, 170
Manchester
  Corporation 3–4
Manchester Literary
  and Philosophical
  Society 9, 10
Manchester
  Metropolitan
  University 12
Manchester School of
  Art 170
Mantle, the Earth's
  69–70

Martineau, Harriet 16,
  131–133, 135, 143–
  155, 162, 163, 168,
  170, 173, 186–187,
  191, 195, 200
Martineau, James 168
Mary Queen of Scots
  115
Mayburgh Henge 99
Mediobogdum 105
Mendeleev, Dmitri 10
mesmerism 146–147,
  148, 153
Mesolithic Age 96–97
metallic minerals,
  deposition of 74–77
metamorphic rocks
  80, 86, 94
meteorology, study of
  9, 64, 201
Mickleden Beck 93, 99
Mid-Atlantic ridge 70
Middle Stone Age
  96–97
Mill, John Stuart 47
Millais, John Everett
  141, 160–161, 169
Millward, Roy 110,
  181–182
mining for metals 65,
  75–77, 167, 180
Monbiot, George
  181–183
Moore, Annie 172
Moore, Noel 173
Montague, Basil 44
moraines, glacial 93
Morris, William 161,
  164
Mosse, Kate 154
Mount St Helen's 72

mountain building 70, 74, 79–87
Mull, Isle of 85
Murray, John 133

national parks, creation of 178–180
National Trust, The 57–58, 166, 171, 176, 180
Near Sawrey 174
Neolithic Age 95–98, 110, 123, 181
Nether Stowey, Somerset 27
Nethermost Cove 85
Nevill, John Cranstoun 154–155
New College, Manchester 9
New Stone Age 95–98
Newcastle upon Tyne 146
Newlands Valley 75
Newton, Isaac 18
Nicholson, Norman 183
Nightingale, Florence 146, 148, 155
nitrous oxide *see* laughing gas
Norman Conquest 108–109, 111–114
Norsemen 110–112
Northumbria, kingdom of 108
Norwich 143, 145

Old Man of Coniston 58, 94, 123, 133, 137

Old Norse words 112
opium 38, 41, 43–44
Ordovician Skiddaw Group 70
Orrest Head 137–138
Otley, Jonathan 63–67, 77, 94, 196, 197–198, 200–201
Ottery St Mary 20
Oxenholme 118
Oxford, University of 41, 48, 158, 161, 171

Pantisocracy 26–27
Pardshaw 7
Parish, Charles 102
Patterdale 136
Peak District National Park 179
Pennington 108
Penrith 22, 23, 25, 106–108, 111, 119
Penruddock 108
periodic table 10
Peter Rabbit (Beatrix Potter character) 169, 172–173, 188, 189
Petrichor 16
Picts 107
picturesque, the 122–125, 134
Pike o' Stickle 98
pollution, lake 61
Pooley Bridge 15
Postman Pat books 195
Potter, Beatrix 76, 141, 168–178, 181, 187–190, 192
Potter, Bertram 168
Potter, Edmund 170

Potter, Rupert 141, 168
Pre-Raphaelites 160
Preston 4
pyroclastic eruptions 72–74

Quakers 7, 143

Racedown Lodge, Dorset 26, 27
Radcliffe, Ann 124–126
railways, arrival of the 118–119, 131, 166–167, 175
rain 14–17
rainfall statistics 14–15
Ramsden, James 57
Ransome, Arthur 57, 75, 190–192
Ravenglass 104–105, 107
Rawnsley, Canon Hardwicke 171–172, 175–176
Rawnsley, Edward Preston 171
reason, human 8
Rebanks, James 182–184
Red Tarn 37, 85
Reich, David 100–101
reivers 115–116
reservoirs 2–4, 107
'rewilding' 180–181, 184–185
Rheged, kingdom of 108
Robert the Bruce 115

Robinson, Adrian 110, 181–182
Robinson, Elihu 7
Robinson, Henry Crabb 148
Rocket, steam locomotive 117–118
Roger of Poitou 114
Roman roads 105–107, 123
Romans in Cumbria 104–108
Romantic Movement 17, 19, 29–30, 50, 121, 156
Rosthwaite 112
Rothay, River 52, 106, 147, 195, 200
Rovelli, Carlo 9
Royal Institution lectures 18, 35
Ruskin College, Oxford 165
Ruskin, John 3, 157–168, 171, 176
Rydal Mount 44–46, 148, 196
Rydal Water 52, 54, 114

Saxons 108–111
Scafell Pike 62, 63, 91, 94, 100, 126
science 8, 11, 35, 132
scientific attitude 8
Scotland, tours of 35, 141, 157, 160
Scots (people) 107
Scott, Sir George Gilbert 200
Scott, Sir Walter 35, 37, 47, 116

Scout Scar, Kendal 83
Scroggs Cottage 64, 196
sea level, changes in 90, 100
Seagrave, Sir Henry 55
Seathwaite 14
Seathwaite Tarn 54
Sedgwick, Professor Adam 65–66, 131
Setantii, the 103
Severn, Joan 165
Sharp Edge 92
Shap Priory 113
Sheffield Clarion Ramblers 179–180
Shelepina, Evgenia Petrovna 191–192
Shepherd, Nan 200
Silver How 92
Skelwith Bridge 195, 196
Skiddaw 22, 46, 63–64, 70, 100, 123, 125
Skiddaw slate 64, 70, 77, 80, 85–86, 94, 100
Skye, Isle of 85
Smith, Ali 154
Smith, Bill 56
Solway Firth 80
Southey, Edith *née* Fricker 27, 35–36, 48
Southey, Robert 21, 26–29, 35–36, 38, 40, 42, 45–46, 48–49, 64, 66, 128, 157, 171, 186–187
Stainton 109
Staveley 26

St John's Beck 2, 3
St John's College, Cambridge 23
St Osyth, Essex 14
Stephenson, Robert 117
Stickle Tarn 92
Stone Age 96–100
stone axes 98–99, 105
stone circles 99–101
stone henges 99–100
Storm Desmond 15
stratigraphy of the Lake District 63, 65
striation lines 91
Striding Edge 37, 88, 92
sublime, the 19–20, 123, 198
Swallows and Amazons 57, 190, 192
Swindale 112
Swinside 112
Swinside stone circle 102

tarns 54, 91–92, 112, 200 *see also individual tarns*
Taylor, Reverend William 23
Tectonic plates 69, 79, 81–82, 84, 85–86
Thirlmere 2–3, 53, 65, 72
Thirlmere aqueduct 4–5
Thompson, Ian 117
Thompson, James 117
Threlkeld, Elizabeth 22, 25

Todd, Barbara 143, 206
Todd Crag 106, 195
trap topography 94
Trease, Geoffrey 194–195
trilobites 68
Trotsky, Leon 191
Troutbeck 4, 93
tuffs, volcanic 73–74
Turner, J.M.W. 19, 156, 159, 160
Tynemouth 146, 186
Tyson, Mrs 23

'U'-shaped valleys 92–93
Ullswater 16, 38, 53, 128, 150, 159, 201
Ullswater Steamers 58–59
Ulverston 113
UNESCO World Heritage Site 180
Unitarian Manchester College 168
Unitarianism 144, 149, 170
United Utilities 4
Upper Borrowdale Volcanics 72–3, 88, 94

Vallon, Annette 24, 25, 32–33
Vallon, Caroline 24, 25, 32–33
Variscan orogeny 83
Vickers Shipbuilding and Engineering (BAE Systems) 57
Victoria, Queen 145

Vikings 108, 110–112, 184
volcanic lavas 71–78, 85
volcanoes 69–78, 85

Wainwright, Alfred 5, 15, 135–142, 143, 183
Wainwright, Betty 139, 141, 142
Wainwright, Peter 138–139, 142
Wainwright, Ruth 141
Wansfell Pike 60, 106
Ward, George 180
Ward, Mary 193
Warne, Frederick 172–173
Warne, Norman 173–174
Wasdale 194
Wastwater 53, 61, 72, 195
water speed records 55–56
Waterloo, Battle of 46
weather readings 9, 12, 64
Wellcome Trust Centre for Human Genetics 111
West, Thomas 121–122
Weston 6
Wetherlam 115, 197
Whitehouse, John 165
Wilde, Oscar 191
Wilkinson, Reverend Joseph 127
William I, King 112

William 'Rufus' II, King 113, 114
Williams, Raymond 184
Wilson, Francis 42
Windermere 1, 52–54, 58–61, 63, 93, 106, 118, 128, 131, 137, 147, 150, 171, 190
Windermere Permanent LandBuilding and Investment Association 150
Windermere Sedimentaries 64
Windermere Supergroup of rocks 78, 94
Wood, Mary 127
Wolfram 76
Wordsworth, Catherine 40, 44
Wordsworth, Dora 40, 47, 52
Wordsworth, Dorothy 16, 21, 22, 25–27, 30, 59, 148–149, 200
Wordsworth, John (WW's father) 22
Wordsworth, John (WW's brother) 32
Wordsworth, John (WW's son) 35, 40, 46
Wordsworth, Mary née Hutchinson, 26, 32–34, 39, 50–52, 57, 59, 147, 148–149, 200

Wordsworth, Thomas
40, 44
Wordsworth, William
8, 14, 16–17, 18,
20–52, 59, 61,
66–67, 109, 110,
118, 126–131, 135,
143, 148–149, 150,
154, 157, 158, 164,
166, 171, 179, 198,
199, 200
Wordsworth, William
(WW's son) 40
Workington 109
Worthington, John
Hugh 144
Wray Castle 171
Wright, Frank Lloyd
164
Wrynose Pass 105
Wythburn 3, 65

Yewthwaite mine 76
Yorkshire College of
Science 190, 192

THE AUTHOR

David Howe OBE is the author of numerous books relating to his academic career. His interests include walking, a layman's interest in science, and his twin passions of geology – which he studied at undergraduate level – and writing. His first non-academic book, which was on walking, was shortlisted for the East Anglian Book Awards. Born and brought up in Manchester, he has a lifelong love of the Lake District.